Contents

Executive Summary

© RAY QUAY

In the face of increasing complexity and uncertainty, planners, public officials, and community residents need new tools to anticipate and shape the future. This report examines the current state of scenario planning and scenario planning tools that can help communities and regions prepare for that future through a variety of visioning, land use, transportation, and other planning efforts. It approaches this topic as an opportunity for using open source software and processes to foster the development, better understanding, and use of these tools.

Decisions about the future are often controversial due to competing economic interests, different cultural values, and divergent views about property rights and the role of government. Broader and more effective civic engagement is needed to ensure community support for decisions about development and other land-related policies and public investments. The traditional predict-and-plan paradigm is inadequate to address all of these challenges. We need to move toward developing and implementing planning tools and processes that foster anticipation and adaptation.

Scenario planning is a promising method to help communities respond to these challenges. It deals with a range of potential futures, whether for regional visioning, comprehensive planning, or project site planning, and provides decision makers, experts, and the public better and more comprehensible information on what these futures might mean for their communities. However, despite their potential, scenario planning tools have not been employed widely for a number of reasons.

Three concepts are considered to be critical to the scenario planning and tool-building process: collaboration, capacity building, and creation of an open environment for engagement. Collaborative problem solving facilitates resolution of interrelated issues that cannot be resolved by one organization alone. Capacity building is needed to enable individuals and organizations to apply scenario planning methods and tools effectively to their specific planning concerns. An open environment for information sharing and education will help accelerate the use and improvement of scenario planning tools in multiple settings.

The Lincoln Institute of Land Policy and Sonoran Institute, with other partners, have convened a community of software developers, planners, and other tool users concerned with the advancement of scenario planning. Participants in our recent workshops concluded that future efforts should focus on five key opportunities: increasing understanding and acceptance of scenario planning; overcoming the complexity and cost of tools; improving access to existing data; enhancing interoperability among different tools; and creating mechanisms to integrate foresight and anticipation into planning processes and implementation.

The emergence of new and improved scenario planning tools over the last 10 years offers promise that the use of scenario planning can increase and that the goal of providing open access to the full potential of scenario planning tools is within reach. This report recommends seven immediate actions that are either in process or could be implemented quickly to facilitate this goal. A community of tool developers and users is already working on various related efforts under the umbrella of the Consortium for Scenario Planning; *www.scenarioplanning.io* is the online host for this initiative.

- **Create an online platform** to foster collaboration in the development and application of scenario planning tools.

- **Develop a curriculum** on scenario planning for the next generation of professional and citizen planners.

- **Establish a model process** for conducting scenario planning and show how it can be used with existing community planning processes.

- **Illustrate different uses of scenario planning tools** in various stages of the planning process to facilitate increased use of scenario planning.

- **Establish data standards** to improve information sharing, starting with development and place types for land use patterns.

- **Initiate a model collaborative project** to demonstrate the potential for integrated tools, models, and modules.

- **Advance new concepts** of anticipatory governance by using foresight and anticipation to address uncertainty and future challenges.

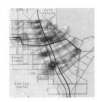

CHAPTER 1

Scenario Planning's Potential

© DESIGN CENTRE FOR SUSTAINABILITY, UNIVERSITY OF BRITISH COLUMBIA, VANCOUVER.

Residents participate in a design charrette in North Vancouver.

Planning for the future of the places we inhabit has become increasingly challenging. The social, economic, environmental, and infrastructure systems that sustain us have become more complex and interdependent, and uncertainty about future changes remains high. A deeper understanding of sustainability has extended the planning horizon to 50 years and beyond, far longer than the terms of most politicians and the careers of today's planners and administrators.

Communities, cities, and regions across the country face a wide range of concerns in making their places more sustainable, and responding to these challenges often requires anticipating future conditions and making decisions about a community's policy options, community services, and infrastructure investments. Such decisions may be controversial because of competing economic interests, differing cultural values, and divergent political views on issues such as property rights and the role of government. In recent years these conflicts have become even more acute. Consequently, broader and more effective civic engagement is needed to ensure community support for decisions about development policies and investments in a community's future.

Decision makers generally seek simplicity in the process of public policy development, but this is difficult to achieve in an environment of complexity, uncertainty, long-term planning horizons, and broad civic engagement. Over the last few decades scenario planning has emerged as a promising method to help decisions makers and the public respond to these challenges. Tools that facilitate the use and analysis of scenarios have not been widely employed, although they have the potential to inform a large number of planning activities. This report explores ways to expand the development and effective use of scenario planning by opening up access to the tools for both users and tool developers.

THE GOAL OF SCENARIO PLANNING

Complexity and uncertainty need not be barriers to planning the long-term future. While it is impossible to optimize for every possible beneficial outcome or feasible future, scenario planning is designed to put better information about alternative futures in the hands of decision makers, experts, and the public. Emerging methods and tools can enable new approaches to planning that were not even envisioned by the profession a decade ago (figure 1).

The goal of scenario planning is to provide a comprehensive view of the inter-related pros and cons of potential futures by breaking out of traditional decision-making silos. As uncertainty increases and available resources decrease, it becomes more important to consider the full range of emerging conditions and the community's ability to adopt policies and pursue investments that will be resilient across a variety of potential futures. Scenario planning is an effective way to specify and assess these futures, whether for regional visioning, comprehensive planning, or project site planning (Kwartler and Longo 2008).

KEY CONCEPTS

Three concepts are recognized as being critical to the scenario planning and tool-building process: collaboration, capacity building, and creation of an open environment for engagement.

FIGURE 1
A Possible Scenario for a Downtown Transit Stop in Superstition Vistas in Arizona

Source: Fregonese Associates, Inc.

Collaboration

Collaborative problem solving facilitates resolution of interrelated issues that previously seemed too complex for one organization to resolve alone. An important aspect of collaboration is inclusive and authentic dialogue that augments individual and organizational capacity to engage in collective problem solving (Innes and Booher 2010).

Knowledge of the problem at hand and the shared values and ideas of other stakeholders increases the collective ability to innovate and achieve solutions. Another element of effective collaboration is the provision of open access to information for all stakeholders and a forum where engagement and dialogue is open to all.

The types of organizations and individuals that need to participate in this process can be grouped into several categories, with the recognition that some individuals may identify with more than one group.

- **Scenario planning and tool advocates:** Organizations and individuals interested in furthering the use of scenario planning and scenario planning tools through outreach, funding, and other activities;
- **Tool developers:** Planning firms, universities, nonprofit organizations, or software developers who are writing, selling, and supporting software for scenario planning;
- **Professional and citizen planners:** Government agencies, organizations, and individuals using scenario planning and scenario planning tools within public planning processes; and
- **Academic educators and researchers:** Faculty and researchers working, studying, and conducting research to advance scenario planning tools within a university, private consulting firm, or nonprofit organization.

Capacity Building

Scenario planning is a not an end in itself, but rather a general method used within a larger planning context to address community or regional issues. The current capacity of planning professionals to apply scenario planning is often limited by their lack of knowledge of the method and limited access to the available tools. Scenario planning continues to evolve as new techniques are developed in public policy practice that draw on research in fields beyond regional and community planning, such as climate change adaptation and water resource management. A transfer of knowledge and expertise from these and related fields is needed to incorporate these new techniques into community and regional planning and to adapt the current generation of scenario planning tools for future situations.

Significant resources, including time, data, expertise, and funds, are also required to use the scenario planning processes and tools discussed in this report. The capacity of organizations and individuals to use scenario planning processes and tools is a function of the knowledge of those involved and the ability of the organization to commit resources to the effort. Enhancing the capacity of users, organizations, and tool developers through an open environment of information sharing and education will accelerate and improve their use over time.

Open Source Environment

The full potential for collaboration and capacity building is not likely to be realized in the same environment that gave rise to existing scenario planning tools. Their development over the last decade has been in a closed environment, with each tool carving out its own, often proprietary, market. Interaction among users occurred primarily among those using a particular scenario planning tool or underlying geographic information system (GIS) platform. This approach is inadquate to address the challenges involved in expanding the use of scenario planning and scenario planning tools. Collaboration is now being facilitated by Internet-enabled tools that create open environments for authentic dialogue, changing the model for advancing science and policy (Nielsen 2012).

One concept that has been demonstrated to create environments of open collaboration and capacity building is known as "open source." In software development, where it originated, this concept means that a group openly collaborates to create a product or service, which is then made freely available to all. In the case of software, this also involves open access to the underlying source code of the program, hence the terms "open" and "source."

Many people who use "free" software such as Wikipedia and Mozilla Firefox are familiar with open source products. Yet, open source embodies more than specific products. It is a way of thinking and approaching complex problems, predicated on the idea that a better result can be forged through collaboration and exchange rather than through traditional production methods (box 1, p. 8). In simple terms, open source is about a share-and-share-alike philosophy that can be applied to both the development of scenario planning tools and the approach taken to solve community and regional problems.

Many in the planning field are familiar with case studies and best practices, and the concept of compiling them is, at its root, similar to open source collaboration and

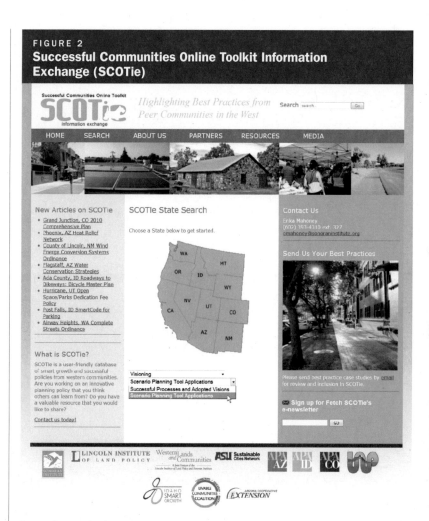

FIGURE 2
Successful Communities Online Toolkit Information Exchange (SCOTie)

Source: Sonoran Institute.

standards. Communities, institutions, and firms disseminate successes and failures so that others can learn, modify, and adapt. The Successful Communities Online Toolkit (Sonoran Institute 2012) is such an example (figure 2). Ideally, these lessons would be shared through both physical and virtual networks. In addition, a tool that allows others to comment and improve on planning problem statements, methods, data, and best practices, and then makes these refinements available to all users, is one of many potential outcomes in applying open source thinking to planning problems.

BOX 1
Open Source Thinking

The core concept of open source is the freedom to obtain and modify the source code of existing software and carry out the creation of new software and tools through an open, collaborative process. Technology provides the functionality to facilitate collaboration over distance and time, while online bug tracking and automated testing and code conflict resolution make it easier to build open source tools. An open source approach, however, does not mean the software is "free." The costs of software maintenance and installation, data management, training, and staffing continue to fall primarily on the user. Related to GIS applications, examples of such development environments are MapWindows, OsGeo, and Open Geospatial Consortium.

People are the most important aspect of open source efforts because the intellectual capital of programmers, coders, tinkerers, designers, and users provides the resources required to build software collaboratively. In addition, legal frameworks in the form of special open source licenses allow participants to clearly understand the use of intellectual contributions and provide rules that guard against unfair use or misuse. A technical background is not necessary to be an open source contributor. In fact, feedback and requests from nontechnical users provide important guidance to improve tools and enhance the user experience.

Open source thinking does not eliminate the need for proprietary systems, nor does it discourage innovation or devalue proprietary tools; rather it helps to improve them. Proprietary systems can participate in and benefit from an environment of collaboration, particularly through the adoption of consistent data input and output standards and improved interoperability among different software tools. Additionally, open source efforts can significantly increase the points of interaction with tools for new users and developers, thus benefiting both open source and proprietary systems.

Software provided at no cost under an open source license need not eliminate financial benefits from supporting, enhancing, and distributing such software. Open source approaches can actually generate economic value through service models that allow tool developers and consultants to charge for value added around open source software, as well as increase returns to proprietary products through the secondary effects of increasing the number and diversity of users (Krishnamurthy 2005; Riehle 2007).

More broadly, open source approaches and thinking help participants succeed in an environment that promotes further adoption of scenario planning practice and enlarges the role for open source and proprietary tools. Experience indicates that an open source approach to tool interoperability and access to data can increase the relevance, adoption, and usability of all scenario planning tools, as well as knowledge about the strengths and appropriate market niches of the different tools.

CHAPTER 2
Scenario Planning Practice

FIGURE 3
Estimates of Greenhouse Gas Reductions Based on Alternative Land Use Options in Seattle, Washington

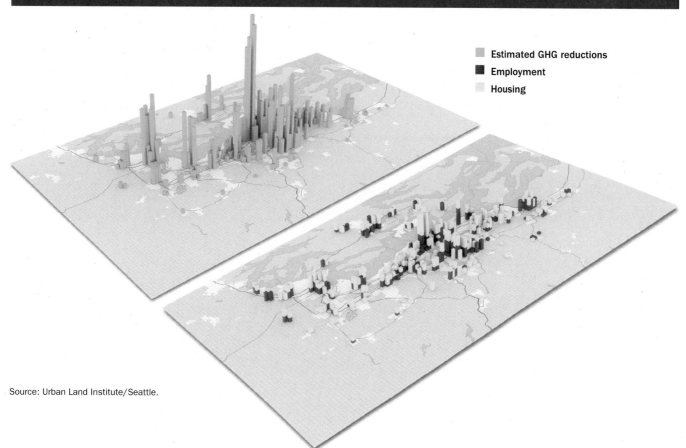

■ Estimated GHG reductions
■ Employment
□ Housing

Source: Urban Land Institute/Seattle.

S cenario planning methods have been used in the business community since the 1960s, but their application for urban and regional planning has been inconsistent (Hopkins and Zapata 2007). Over the last decade, however, scenario planning has begun to flourish, fueled by widely recognized successes, such as Envision Utah and other regional initiatives; by increasing uncertainty in social, economic, and environmental systems; and by faster computing, advances in visualization software, and increased availability of GIS and other data necessary to model these systems (figure 3).

Scenario planning today is being used to address a variety of planning issues across a wide range of scales, from large-scale natural resource management to the evaluation of project site designs. In fact, scenario planning is now a required part of some public planning processes, including legislatively mandated greenhouse gas (GHG) reduction planning in California and Oregon and U.S. Department of Housing and Urban Development (HUD) grants for community sustainability. Scenario planning processes can vary substantially based on the issue being addressed, the institutions conducting the planning, and the information and resources available.

This report focuses on scenario planning used with community and regional visioning, land use, transportation, and other planning efforts. Scenario planning in this context is frequently facilitated with GIS sketch planning tools that allow the development and analysis of land use and transportation scenarios.

THE USES AND USERS OF SCENARIOS

Urban and regional scenario planning today falls on a continuum between two types of scenario planning: normative and exploratory. Normative scenario planning is used to articulate the values of a community or region by eliciting people's opinions about different possible visions of the future (Hopkins and Zapata 2007).

Comparing the pros and cons of several scenarios allows a variety of values to be identified, in order to derive a common set of values or goals for the future of the community or region. In this type of planning the scenarios are frequently applied to major policy decisions that could have a substantial impact on the future form of the community, such as funding and locating transportation infrastructure or changing land use regulations. Each scenario is based on how the future may play out under a different policy approach.

Groups of scenarios are often bookended by scenarios that represent a range between least and most aggressive actions relative to a baseline "business-as-usual" or "no action" alternative. Assessment of the impacts of each scenario on indicators such as traffic congestion, infrastructure costs, air quality, open space, or affordable housing can help

people articulate the pros and cons of each impact, and thus begin to articulate values and goals for the future. This is the type of scenario planning that has been used most commonly by local and regional planners and was notably successful in the Envision Utah planning process.

The second type, exploratory scenario planning, is used to anticipate the impact that different future conditions may have on values, policies, or goals that have been established or are being considered (Weber 2006). The desired end result of such a process is a set of robust or contingent strategies that policy makers can use to achieve agreed-upon goals under a wide variety of possible but uncertain futures. These scenarios are typically based on changes in environmental, social, or economic factors that could affect the future of the community, yet are beyond local control, such as aging of the population, the state of the economy, population growth rates, and climate change.

Each scenario is based on a different possible end state of one or more of these factors, which are often selected to represent the full range of possible future conditions. Assessment of how each scenario affects the community's ability to achieve its goals can be used to identify how potential change can create opportunities or threats and determine what strategies can be used to avoid undesired changes or promote desired outcomes.

The scenario planning tools described in this report are found within the full range of the continuum between normative and exploratory. They are used to develop land use and transportation scenarios at a range of scales, engage the public in participatory planning processes, and create visualizations for values and goal setting. The scenarios may be related to a desired community form, such as maximizing growth around

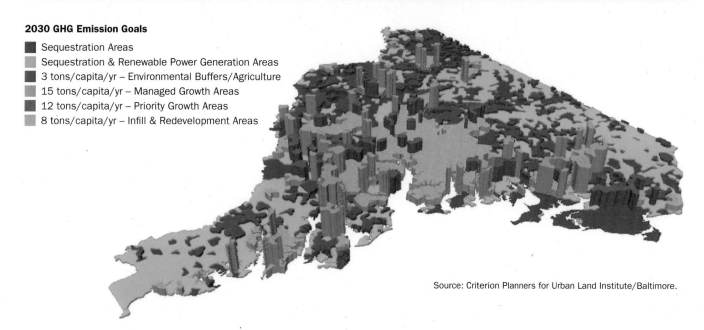

FIGURE 4
2030 GHG Emissions Goals for Baltimore, Maryland

2030 GHG Emission Goals

- Sequestration Areas
- Sequestration & Renewable Power Generation Areas
- 3 tons/capita/yr – Environmental Buffers/Agriculture
- 15 tons/capita/yr – Managed Growth Areas
- 12 tons/capita/yr – Priority Growth Areas
- 8 tons/capita/yr – Infill & Redevelopment Areas

Source: Criterion Planners for Urban Land Institute/Baltimore.

transit, identifying development and redevelopment opportunities, testing and refining regional transportation plans, or developing strategies for climate change mitigation and adaptation (figure 4). Exploratory scenario planning is expected to become more important for developing sustainable approaches to address increasing uncertainty.

The following sections describe three types of scenario planning users. The associated case examples introduce four specific tools that are described in more detail in chapter 3: CommunityViz, Envision Tomorrow, INDEX, and I-PLACE³S.

City and County Users
Scenario planning uses within city and county planning activities include:
- comprehensive and area planning;
- transit corridor and station planning;
- neighborhood planning;
- infrastructure (water, sewer, street, and storm) planning;
- project impact assessment;
- climate change mitigation and adaptation strategies development; and
- regulatory analysis.

For comprehensive and regional plans, a variety of existing tools are available to engage the public in a workshop setting or to develop scenarios of different development alternatives. The scenarios help test policies and prioritize strategies. Scenarios can also be utilized to demonstrate to stakeholders how key future conditions could impact their community and to consider which approaches may be most robust across a variety of potential future conditions. After a plan is completed, scenario planning tools can be used to monitor the plan's status during implementation.

At a smaller scale, scenario planning tools can be used to develop and analyze design alternatives at a site plan or building scale for neighborhoods or transit stations and corridors. They can also be used to understand the infrastructure capacity and demand timing implications of different land uses in the future. In addition, these tools can be used to explore the implications of various zoning assumptions or proposals when rezoning or optimizing a community's zoning code is being considered.

FIGURE 5
Land Use Palette for Scenario Sketching in Elburn, Illinois

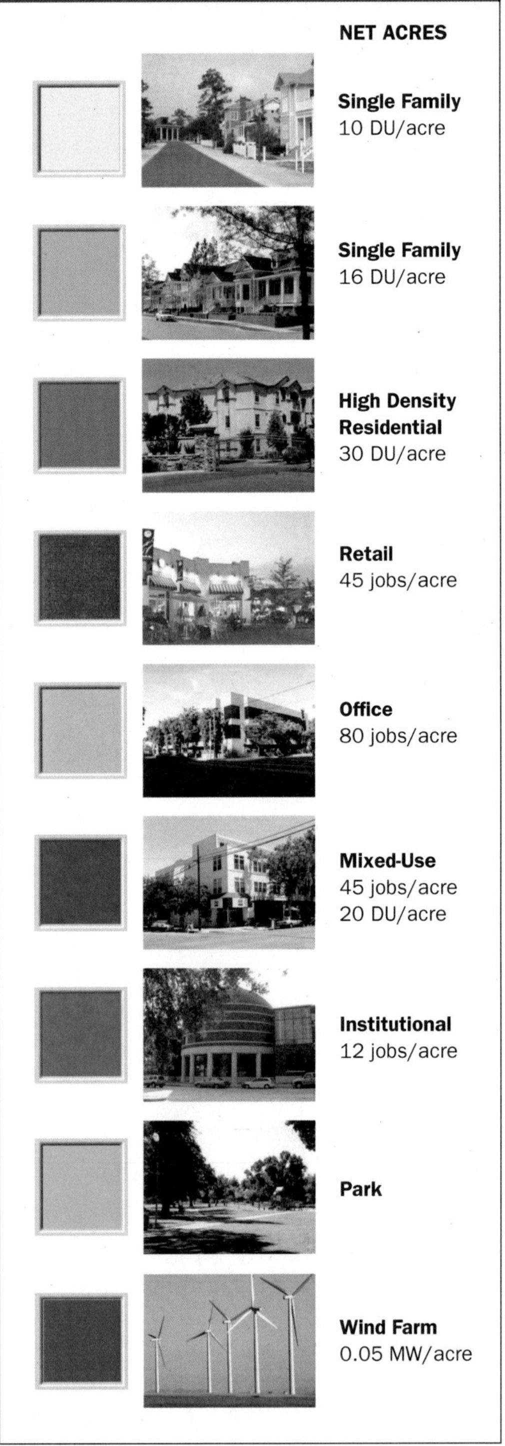

NET ACRES

Single Family
10 DU/acre

Single Family
16 DU/acre

High Density
Residential
30 DU/acre

Retail
45 jobs/acre

Office
80 jobs/acre

Mixed-Use
45 jobs/acre
20 DU/acre

Institutional
12 jobs/acre

Park

Wind Farm
0.05 MW/acre

DU=Dwelling Units   MW= Megawatts

Source: Criterion Planners; Condon, Cavens, and Miller (2008, 22).

Transit Station Area, Elburn, Illinois

Elburn, Illinois, with a population of approximately 4,000, is located about 50 miles west of downtown Chicago. The Metra commuter rail system extended a rail line to the community in 2005, with a station about four or five blocks from Elburn's downtown. In 2004, in anticipation of the rail station, the Urban Land Institute and the Campaign for Sensible Growth organized a technical assistance panel that worked with the community to identify strategies to accommodate inevitable growth while protecting the community's sense of place and lifestyle.

One recommendation was to encourage transit-oriented development (TOD) on a 300-acre site southeast of the station. This site is now one of the community's focus areas for future growth. Elburn used INDEX in a full-day digital charrette in which 60 residents and officials sketched alternative plans for a TOD site. Each alternative was analyzed for its impact on the community. Important design goals in using the tool in this context were to maintain the small block street grid of the adjacent historic downtown and to protect wetlands on the site as part of the community's "emerald necklace" of parks and streams that ring the downtown (figure 5).

Comprehensive Plan, Grand Junction, Colorado

In 2007, the City of Grand Junction initiated a process to update its comprehensive plan, using CommunityViz as part of the public engagement process. The city hosted 27 citizen planner "chip games" during which residents used "chips" to indicate on a map where and at what density they would like to see growth occur. The need for compact development was a theme echoed in each game. The results were collected, digitized, and analyzed with CommunityViz, and then shared with the public in subsequent workshops. As alternative land use plans were developed during the process, CommunityViz could dynamically update information into the regional database to allow the testing of impacts on the transportation system. This iterative process eventually revealed a preferred alternative scenario, and Grand Junction's comprehensive plan was adopted in 2010.

Metropolitan Planning Organization Users

Many scenario planning tools have been developed to respond to regional growth challenges, and thus are particularly well-suited to planning on a large scale. Metropolitan planning organizations (MPOs) tend to use these tools to encompass a geography beyond individual cities and counties. Examples include regional transportation plans (RTPs), integrated regional land use and transportation plans, regional visioning, and plans to reach GHG reduction targets. The tools are frequently linked with other models operated by MPOs, such as economic models, transportation models, and infrastructure models.

Blueprint, Sacramento Area Council of Governments

In 2003, the Sacramento Area Council of Governments (SACOG) launched an award-winning regional growth analysis called Blueprint. The analysis of six counties is based on a broad partnership of regional stakeholders including employers, developers, investors, the press, special interest groups, and citizens. I-PLACE³S, an Internet-based planning tool, was used to help SACOG work with elected officials and the public in dozens of interactive planning workshops. I-PLACE³S was used during the workshops to provide real-time information about how different growth alternatives would affect the region's transportation system, air quality, housing, and natural resource protection, among other issues. Output from I-PLACE³S was also used as input to the SACOG regional travel model to estimate the impact of land use alternatives on travel and the transportation network. The result was a preferred Blueprint Scenario that is used by SACOG with I-PLACE³S as a comparative scenario to review development proposals for its member agencies (figure 6).

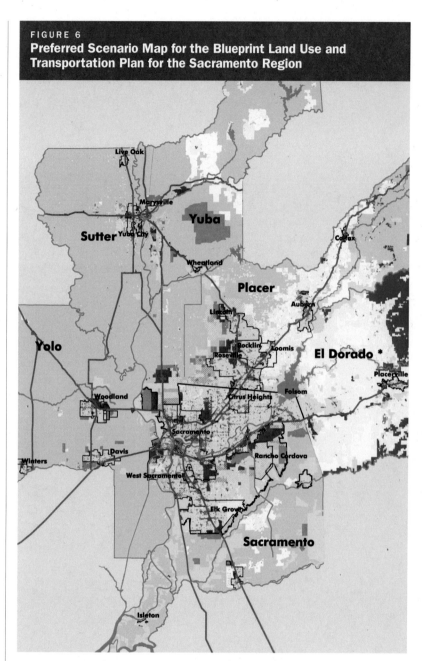

FIGURE 6
Preferred Scenario Map for the Blueprint Land Use and Transportation Plan for the Sacramento Region

Note: El Dorado County was not able to directly participate in the Blueprint project that led to the SACOG Board's adoption of the 2050 Blueprint concept map and growth principles. The land use pattern shown on this map represents SACOG's expected growth in El Dorado County through 2035, the planning horizon year of the next Metropolitan Transportation Plan. For the other five counties in the SACOG region this map represents Blueprint growth through 2050.

Source: Sacramento Area Council of Governments.

Conceptual Land Use Scenario, Southern California Association of Governments

The Conceptual Land Use Scenario (CLUS) was developed for Southern California Association of Governments (SCAG) in response to the passage of Assembly Bill 32 (AB 32), which requires California to reduce statewide carbon emissions to 1990 levels by the year 2020, and Senate Bill 375 (SB 375), which calls for coordinated, regional land use and transportation planning to help reduce the state's total carbon emissions. Because the region had to go beyond existing policy to meet the anticipated carbon emissions reduction target, SCAG decided to explore how far land use planning could go toward reducing regional vehicle miles traveled. SCAG used Envision Tomorrow to isolate specific land use planning principles known to reduce trips—such as increased density, mixed land uses, and focused growth around transit areas—to evaluate how such changes might impact transportation patterns and reduce regional emissions.

Nonprofit, Business, and Community Users

Nonprofit, business, and community organizations at local and regional levels are taking a larger role in planning as they represent interests as diverse as environmental protection, community health, and social equity. These organizations often use scenarios to advocate for their interests and ensure that their values are represented in decisions that will guide local and regional growth. Many of them also use scenario planning tools to test alternatives and assert their positions within community planning processes. Some nonprofit organizations, such as the Sonoran Institute, work directly with local jurisdictions to build technical capacity to encourage the use of these tools.

Supporting Youth in Designing Sustainable Neighborhoods, Boston, Massachusetts

A group of university and educational partners used CommunityViz for a program in which 200 Boston-area high school students worked on projects related to urban planning and sustainability. Students engaged in field studies before they began building and comparing neighborhood-scale scenarios in their weekly courses and intensive one-to-two-week-long workshops.

Superstition Vistas, Arizona

Superstition Vistas, a 275-square-mile tract of undeveloped state trust land in Arizona, is one of the largest pieces of land under single ownership in any metropolitan area. Its sensitive location is in the path of the fast-developing Sun Corridor that encompasses the region between Phoenix and Tucson. Envision Tomorrow was used to create six large-scale scenarios, ranging from a trend scenario to a compact, transit-oriented form (figure 7). The scenarios are being used to help guide future decision making about sustainable development for the Superstition Vistas site (Holway 2011).

EMERGING PRACTICE

The scenario planning practices and cases described above attempt to forecast what may happen to regions and communities under different policies that influence urban form and transportation. The goals of these planning efforts are to help communities decide what they want for their future (normative) and how they will achieve these aspirations under different possible future conditions (exploratory). Tool developers acknowledge that the models included in their tools are not intended to create a static prediction of the future; rather they create a reasonable estimation of what might occur given a defined set of assumptions.

Even with advances in the science of systems modeling, the ability to predict the future is tenuous at best (Flyvbjerg, Holm, and Buhl 2005; Lempert and Schlesinger 2000). It is impossible to model all of the functions and details of complex and dynamic social and environmental systems (Cox and Stephenson 2007), and their future is plagued with uncertainty (Brewer 1983;

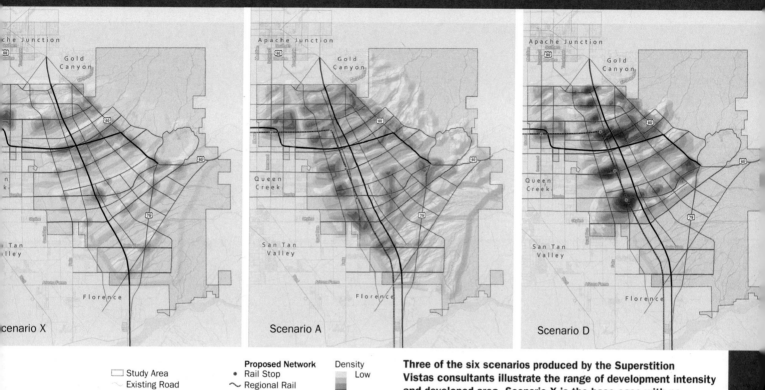

Scenario X

Scenario A

Scenario D

Study Area
Existing Road
Creeks and Washes
Central Arizona Project
100 Year Floodplain

0 0.9 1.8 2.7 Miles
0 5,000 10,000 15,000 Feet

Proposed Network
● Rail Stop
Regional Rail
Freeway
Arizona Parkway
Major Road

Density
Low
Medium
High

Three of the six scenarios produced by the Superstition Vistas consultants illustrate the range of development intensity and developed area. Scenario X is the base case with no comprehensive planning. Scenario A has a minor density increase over current trends in other parts of the region. Scenario D focuses on high-density urban centers.

Source: Superstition Vistas Consulting Team (2011).

Pielke, Sarewitz, and Byerly 2000; Stewart 2000; Waddell 2011). This unpredictability is exacerbated by unanticipated "black swan" events in politics, economics, nature, and technology, such as war and natural disasters, that can radically change the course of human events (Taleb 2007). Although few urban modelers would claim that their work rises to a level of prediction, when citizens are asked to choose a future and a decision path to get there, they are effectively relying on a prediction that following that path will lead to the future of their choice.

Most physical planning today forecasts a future trend or chooses a desired future and then identifies the decisions needed to serve or create that future (Hopkins and Zapata

2007). We are more likely to be able to predict the impacts of policy interventions if social and environmental systems are stationary or change very slowly and the planning horizon is relatively short (20 or fewer years). In addition, the implications of being wrong are less if funding for services and infrastructure is abundant and stable and the consequences of failure are not disastrous. Unfortunately, today we face a number of issues, such as an interdependent global economy, cultural and demographic shifts, climate change, and political schism, which challenge such comfortable assumptions.

It is evident that the traditional planning paradigm of predict-and-plan will not prove adequate to address these and other planning issues that society will face over the next 50 years (Milly et al. 2008; National Research Council 2010). In response, a new model of anticipatory governance in planning practice considers a range of possible futures, prepares strategies to respond to one or more of these futures, and then adapts to those changes as the future unfolds over time (Quay 2010).

The concept of anticipatory governance entails three basic steps:

1. *Use foresight and futures analysis:* Foresight is the act of looking forward to what is possible. Though we cannot predict the future, we can anticipate a wide range of potential future conditions. Different scenarios can be based on expert opinion or developed using models that estimate future conditions across a range of values for one or more factors. These are not normative scenarios to be compared or valued individually; rather they are used in aggregate to explore the sensitivity or risk of various factors (e. g., population, economy, climate) and their range of impacts. Such analysis clarifies uncertainty by helping planners identify and focus on the most important aspects of future possibilities.

2. *Anticipate adaptation:* Using the futures analysis, potential actions to adapt to particular futures are identified. These actions may be important to preserve future options or respond to specific potential changes. Such actions may be flexible, allowing incremental implementation, or they may be robust, working well across a large number of possible futures.

3. *Monitor and adapt:* On a regular basis the factors related to the anticipated futures are monitored to identify changes and the need to respond. As different scenarios become more or less likely, actions anticipated for them can be implemented

or abandoned as appropriate. Given the long time frame for issues such as regional growth and climate change, planning and monitoring time frames can span many decades. Thus educating future decision makers and institutionalizing these concepts is critical.

Most applications of anticipatory governance have occurred in fields tangential to community and regional planning, such as water resource planning, open space conservation, and climate change adaptation. An exception is its use in Urban Land Institute (ULI) Reality Check regional visioning projects in Maryland, Arizona, North Texas, and the Puget Sound area. These tactile exercises use LEGO® bricks to allocate future growth on a game board map. Increasingly, these activities are tied to GIS analysis capabilities to generate multiple stakeholder scenarios (foresight) and scenario analysis methods to create robust regional planning strategies (anticipation).

Vision North Texas, Dallas–Fort Worth, Texas

Vision North Texas (VNT) is a grassroots regional visioning effort organized in 2005 as a public-private-academic partnership among North Central Texas Council of Governments, the North Texas District Council of ULI, and the University of Texas at Arlington. The intent of this effort is to move the region away from a business-as-usual model and toward a more sustainable future. VNT conducted dozens of development principle exercises using LEGO® bricks in different parts of the region, resulting in an ensemble of future urban form scenarios. Analysis revealed a range of perspectives toward the region's future urban form, yet there was consensus about the need for alternatives to inefficient and unsustainable suburban sprawl.

Rather than selecting a single regional vision, VNT crafted four mutually inclusive visions (connected centers, return on investment, diverse distinct

FIGURE 8
Vision North Texas: Preferred Physical Development Pattern for the Year 2050

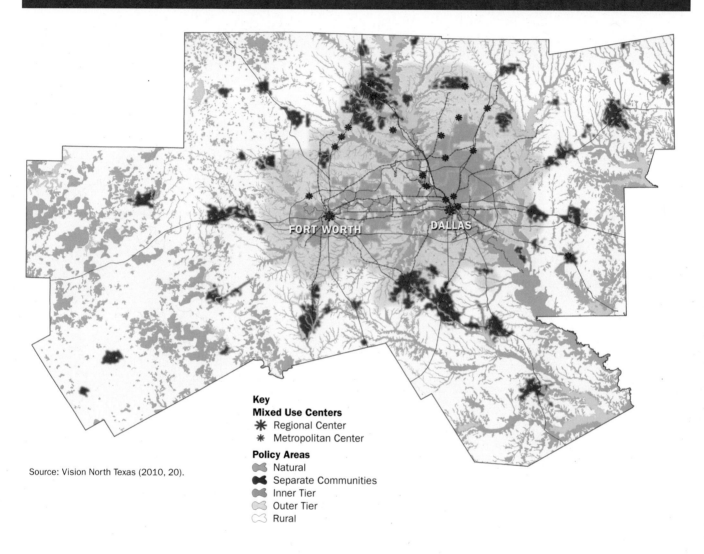

Source: Vision North Texas (2010, 20).

Key

Mixed Use Centers

✳ Regional Center

✴ Metropolitan Center

Policy Areas

Natural

Separate Communities

Inner Tier

Outer Tier

Rural

communities, and green region) that described the range of opinions and options on future urban form. An illustrative diagram of a preferred physical development pattern that embraced these options (figure 8), a set of 12 Guiding Principles, and policy recommendations addressing eight topical investment areas provide flexible guidance for the region's communities to craft sustainable futures that are unique to their location and politics.

SUMMARY

Scenario planning has proven to be an effective method to address complex issues, such as community and regional growth planning, and new approaches are now emerging to help address highly uncertain challenges such as climate change adaptation. A number of specific scenario planning tools have proven effective for facilitating a broad range of planning processes.

CHAPTER 3

Scenario Planning Tools

© FREGONESE ASSOCIATES, INC.

An example of a main street place type in the West Village neighborhood of Dallas, Texas.

The specific types of scenario planning tools examined here are often referred to as sketch planning tools. These computer-based land use evaluation tools are usable at multiple scales, including the site, district, city, and region. They can be applied quickly to illustrate and analyze land use and transportation alternatives based on indicators related to a community's goals and issues.

Users of these tools typically create scenarios of future conditions in their community or region, frequently based on the expected impacts of public policies that will define a future urban form and transportation network. They then use the tool to assess how well each scenario aligns with the community's goals for the future. These tools are a subset of the more general category called planning support systems (PSS) that includes other methodologies such as econometric and agent-based behavioral modeling (Brail 2008).

The scenario planning tools described below are based on a GIS or database system that can use different units of analysis. Traditional tools started at the development or place-type scale, but many of them are now able to support modeling of individual buildings. A development or place-type tool might include a town center or residential neighborhood, while a building-type tool could include a retail store or a single-family home. One potential benefit of starting at the building scale as a unit of analysis is that it can more closely reflect the realities of local urban development patterns. One of the disadvantages in that type of analysis is an increase in the data and setup requirements for the model.

Like all modeling tools, scenario planning tools have limitations. Since they are inherently design-based, users must specify a set of assumptions or parameters. As a result, the scenario outputs are only as sound as the data and assumptions that go into them. Some of the tools are described as "black boxes," with internal calculations that may not be transparent to all users, while others expose these calculations, including both data and assumptions. Nevertheless, the complexity of the combined assumptions, design decisions, and black box calculations means that these tools have the potential to be misunderstood or used incorrectly.

There is no substitute for a thorough and transparent review and understanding of all of the scenario assumptions. Greater transparency of underlying methods can be provided within the software itself (e.g., CommunityViz) or through external documentation (e.g., INDEX). Being able to "show the work" is important for catching errors and increasing the level of trust in the outputs that ultimately will inform decision making. In fact, most of the default assumptions are based on industry expertise or best practices, and the ability to explore changes to the underlying assumptions is an explicit part of the scenario design process.

Scenario planning tools and the uses to which they are being applied have improved considerably since the 1990s (Brail 2008; Condon, Cavens, and Miller 2009). These planning tools have evolved to help professional and citizen planners analyze development options and scenarios, and they may include fiscal impact models; simple local area population allocation models; water and sewer capacity and design models; local storm water and watershed flood models; trip generation models; and general and detailed environmental impact models (figure 9). Some of these tools have been available commercially, while others have been available as free public domain or open source software. Some are based on simple spreadsheets, while others are highly complex dynamic models.

Specialized tools, including UrbanSIM, SLUETH, and What If?, attempt to forecast future patterns of urban growth. They utilize methods such as cellular automata, econometric, and agent-based models to simulate the complex dynamics of land use allocation and development. They share some

FIGURE 9
Connecting 2D and 3D Information to Analyze Urban Conditions in Seattle, Washington

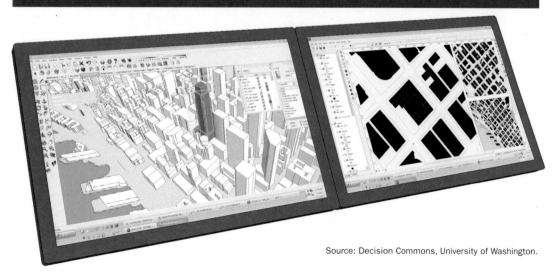

Source: Decision Commons, University of Washington.

TABLE 1

Summary of Scenario Planning Tools

Tool	CommunityViz	Envision Tomorrow	INDEX	I-PLACE³S
Developer	Orton Family Foundation, Middlebury, VT; Placeways, Boulder, CO	Fregonese Associates, Portland, OR (Envision Tomorrow+ to be developed with University of Utah)	Criterion Planners, Portland, OR	Sacramento (CA) Area Council of Governments
Year Developed	2001; 2004–2005	2004	1994	2002
Summary of Approach	Spatial, GIS-based	Spatial, GIS- and Excel-based	Spatial, GIS-based	Spatial, web-based
Scale	Building to regional	Building to regional	Place type to regional	Place type to regional
Open Source Status	Proprietary with open access models	Open source, housed at University of Utah	Proprietary, in transition to open source	Open source
2D Map Visualizations	Yes	Yes	Yes	Yes
3D Visualizations	Yes	No	No	No
Cost	$500 (Self service support) and $850 per user (one year support and upgrades)	There is no cost associated with downloading Envision Tomorrow+.	A standard version of Index PlanBuilder costs $1900.	Contact SACOG
Requirements	Version 4.12, is compatible with ArcGIS 9.2 and up, including 10. Windows XP, Windows Vista, or Windows 7 (with MS .Net Framework 2.0 and DirectX 9.0) is required. A Windows operating system and at least the basic version of ArcGIS Desktop are required.	Requires Windows XP or Vista, MS Office 2000 Pro or greater, and Esri's ArcGIS desktop software 9.3 or greater. The tool supports all ArcGIS license types (ArcView, ArcEditor, and ArcInfo).	Desktop tool requires Windows, MS Office 2000 Pro with Access, and ArcGIS 9.3. Web tool operates on Windows or Linux servers using a PostgreSQL/ PostGIS database and a Python-centric application featuring Django, Mapnik, GEO/OGR, ExtJS, OpenLayers, and GeoExt.	Requires an Internet browser, centralized server, a JAVA virtual engine, and access to an Esri ArcGIS application and license, which EcoInteractive maintains. I-PLACE³S works with both the integrated 4-step travel model that requires a current Citilabs license, as well as any external travel model.

similarities with the tools discussed in this report, though they are much more complex. One distinct difference is that these specialized tools forecast future land use as an output of the model, while most sketch planning tools use a future land use alternative as input. The high-end computational and data needs of some tools can limit their usefulness for sketch planning, but they are frequently used as either a precursor to create alternatives for input into sketch planning tools or to examine sketch tool outputs in more detail.

LEADING SCENARIO PLANNING TOOLS

Four scenario planning tools are used widely today: CommunityViz, Envision Tomorrow, I-PLACE³S, and INDEX. Each of them provides a variety of features and unique capabilities, yet there is substantial overlap among them (table 1).

CommunityViz

CommunityViz is a 3D analysis and planning extension for ArcGIS that provides scenario planning, analysis, and 3D visualization (Walker and Daniels 2011). It was created by the Orton Family Foundation and released in 2001. In 2004–2005, development and operations were spun off into a new company called Placeways, which now markets and develops CommunityViz in partnership with the foundation.

The software helps communities and

regions understand the implications of planning decisions and scenarios. It offers a range of tools for community design and planning, including development of realistic 3D models, build-out analysis, suitability analysis, impact assessment, and growth modeling. Public participation is a key focus, and the software includes numerous features to support public workshops and interactive sessions with diverse audiences. It has been used in conjunction with chip games and electronic meeting tools, and as a facilitation tool to help groups understand and make better planning decisions (figure 10).

Scenario 360, the scenario analysis component, has easy-to-use exploration tools, setup wizards for particular planning applications, standard impact calculations, and a sophisticated geospatial formula engine for creating custom models and analyses. The Common Impacts Wizard can produce up to 16 custom indicators based on user-entered formulas. The Land Use Designer allows land use scenarios to be sketched on a map using predefined or user-customized land use types. Users create their own scenarios for a region or community starting with existing GIS data and then sketch on the map or specify land use policies. Using built-in standard formulas or their own custom models, users measure how scenarios perform relative to user-defined objectives.

A typical Scenario 360 analysis compares the implications of three or four scenarios using dozens or hundreds of indicators displayed in charts, maps, and tables. Weighted factors can be changed to show how different values and priorities impact the final analysis. A real-time update capability allows users to change input settings, assumptions, and weightings, or to edit features on the map and get immediate updates that result from these changes.

Specialized map editing capabilities provide a wide range of sketch modes including place types, chip games, land use "painting" to create different options on a map, and tight integration with ArcGIS templates and sketch tools. Assumptions and values can be changed "on the fly" to update the analysis.

FIGURE 10
CommunityViz Features and Analysis Tools

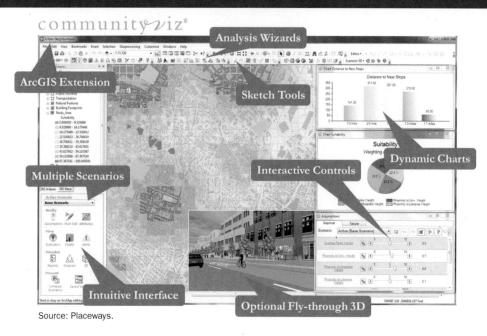

Source: Placeways.

The Build-Out Wizard calculates the development capacity of a scenario. Additional tools are available for growth allocation, suitability and risk analysis, fragmentation and optimization, and other planning functions. CommunityViz models and formulas are open, transparent, editable, and sharable. The tool also has the ability to connect to other tools such as Microsoft Excel or specialized impact models for real-time data sharing and updates.

The Scenario 3D component allows users to build complex, interactive, photo-realistic 3D scenes from two dimensional data, which can be explored with ArcGIS flythrough technology or GoogleEarth, or exported as 3D models in common CAD and SketchUp formats. A ModelBuilder3D component also allows users to generate realistic 3D models of objects such as buildings and trees, or other tools such as SketchUp can be used.

CommunityViz currently provides three different methods of creating realistic 3D models of proposed plans. The GoogleEarth exporter makes .kml files compatible with GoogleEarth, ArcGIS Explorer, and other viewers. Scenario 3D, which comes with CommunityViz, creates very realistic, smaller-scale scenes that use SketchUp building models and can be viewed with a free viewer. An ArcScene extension allows users to work in the ArcGIS 3D environment. Community Viz can be used with, but does not include, an external travel model.

Envision Tomorrow

Envision Tomorrow began as a proprietary toolkit used in the national planning practice of Fregonese Associates, Inc. Over time demand increased for an open source version usable by clients at different scales. At its core, Envision Tomorrow is a Microsoft Excel and ArcGIS-based modeling and evaluation tool that analyses growth and development scenarios at a range of scales from neighborhood to regional.

It utilizes several components to develop and evaluate land use scenarios. The Prototype Builder is able to design buildings and site plans and test their physical and financial feasibility at a local level. It can be used to estimate the physical and financial feasibility of development regulations based on a range of factors including parking, height and use requirements, costs associated with construction, fees, rents, and subsidies.

Although building prototype analysis alone can be used for small-scale site scenarios, the prototypes can also be combined, along with open spaces, streets, and civic uses to create a series of development types, such as main street, mixed-use neighborhood, and strip commercial. The development types then form the basis for land use scenarios at the district, city, county, and regional scale.

With the Scenario Builder component, users can "paint the landscape" to allocate these development types across a study area. This component concurrently allows the creation and comparison of up to five land use scenarios. An Excel-based scenario spreadsheet is dynamically linked to the tool and maintains the scenario outputs such as housing mix in a series of tabs for quick comparison. Changes made to a scenario are automatically reported in the spreadsheet for instant monitoring. Users can focus on small areas for detailed design control or zoom to a larger scenario with the small area changes intact. Detailed scenario results are exportable and reportable at any geography.

Envision Tomorrow has been used to design small single-parcel alternatives for cities such as Tulsa (figure 11), as well as regional scenarios for the Chicago and Southern California areas. It does not include an internal travel model, but is frequently used in conjunction with an external travel model.

Utah's Wasatch Front Regional Council received a Sustainable Communities grant from HUD to fund Envision Tomorrow's move to open source and establish a permanent home at the University of Utah. This grant is also funding the expansion of a set of tools, known as Envision Tomorrow+, which includes 18 modules covering transportation, housing, economics, environment, and other planning elements. The modules are being released as they are completed, with anticipated release dates during 2012 and 2013.

INDEX

INDEX is an integrated suite of desktop and web-based scenario planning tools for neighborhoods, communities, and regions. The tools operate on the desktop as an ArcGIS extension and on the web as an open source application. INDEX was introduced in 1994 by Criterion Planners for land use, transportation, and environmental planners in public agencies and design firms, and for university instructors.

INDEX applications usually begin with benchmark measurements of existing conditions to produce a strengths, weaknesses, opportunities, and threats (SWOT) analysis and create a frame of reference for evaluating alternative futures. The tools are then used to design and visualize scenarios, score their performance, and compare and rank them in terms of goal achievement. Once

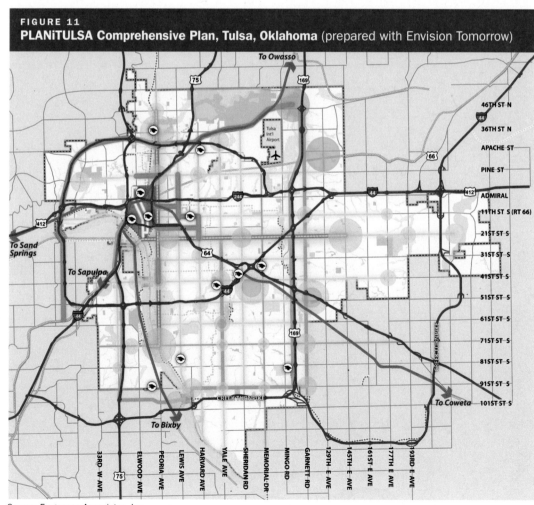

FIGURE 11
PLANiTULSA Comprehensive Plan, Tulsa, Oklahoma (prepared with Envision Tomorrow)

Source: Fregonese Associates, Inc.

FIGURE 12
INDEX Scenario Evaluation Process

① Benchmark Conditions

- Identify strengths & weaknesses
- Set goals

② Sketch Scenarios

- Paint land-uses
- Draw transportation facilities

③ Score Indicators

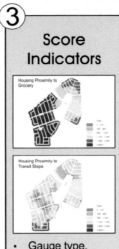

- Gauge type, amount, and location of impacts

④ Rank by Goal Achievement

- Iterate to most goal-responsive alternative

Source: Criterion Planners.

a preferred alternative is selected, its implementation can be evaluated incrementally for goal consistency, and cumulative changes can be measured with periodic progress reports (figure 12).

INDEX uses a database of nested geographies that start at the building level and work up through parcels, census block groups, traffic analysis zones, local government jurisdictions, subregions, and regions. For integrated land use and transportation analyses, it also includes distinct travel networks for walking, biking, transit, and motor vehicles. INDEX scenario planning functions are organized in a series of modules that culminate in a library of 150 indicators that measure scenario performance. This library is organized into measurements of demographics, land use, housing, employment, transportation, environment, energy, and climate protection.

Scenarios can be visualized through use of multimedia presentations and 3D modeling. The modules include:

- Case Designer for creating scenarios in real time with stakeholders participating in digital charrettes;
- an ROI tool for evaluating real estate

development feasibility;
- a fiscal impact tool for assessing local government costs and benefits;
- SGWater for water use and storm water modeling;
- 7Ds for estimating changes in walk, bike, transit, and auto use as a result of land use and urban design actions;
- LEED-ND Connections (Leadership in Energy and Environmental Design for Neighborhood Development) for connectivity analysis using LEED criteria;
- Cool Spots for modeling building and transportation energy use and GHG emissions; and
- a rating and weighting tool for ranking scenarios by goal achievement.

The INDEX open source web tool is designed for practitioners and members of the public who have no special GIS or technical modeling skills. To facilitate rapid set-up and ease of use, it is preloaded with national data sets for the categories listed above. These provide contextual and benchmark information at the census block level. The database can be expanded locally with additional data sets that can reach down to the parcel and building levels. Users are able to assemble scenarios by combining and editing features online or by importing them from the desktop tool. Multiple scenarios can be displayed for public evaluation and preference ranking.

I-PLACE³S

I-PLACE³S (Planning for Community Energy, Economic, and Environmental Sustainability) is a software tool that facilitates integrated land use and transportation scenario planning. This web-based platform creates land use and transportation scenarios, conducts detailed scenario analysis, and engages the public in workshops using place types and other variables (figure 13).

The original PLACE³S software application was a desktop application developed in the late 1990s in the public domain by Parsons Brinckerhoff, Fregonese Associates, Calthorpe Associates, and Space Imaging and in collaboration with Esri. It was funded by the California Energy Commission, the U.S. Department of Energy, the Sacramento Area Council of Governments, the Association of Bay Area Governments, the City of San Diego, the San Diego Association of Governments, the City of Sacramento, the Georgia Regional Transportation Authority, and the California Department of Transportation.

In 2002, the California Energy Commission contracted with EcoInteractive, a software development company, to convert the desktop version of PLACE³S to an Internet version of the land use model, now referred to as I-PLACE³S. The former PLACE³S

FIGURE 13
Sample Building and Place Types for Public Workshops Using I-PLACE³S

Code and Name		Examples	DU/Acre Range	Far Range	Description
Mixed Use Building Types					
RCO	Regional/ Commercial Office		--	0.3–0.4	75% Retail 25% Office
CNCO	Community/Neighborhood Commercial/Office		--	0.2–0.3	75% Retail 25% Office
MU1	Mixed Use Employment Focus		15–25	0.75–1+	45% Residential 40% Retail 15% Office
MU2	Mixed Use Residential Focus		60–90	1.5–2.5	70% Residential 25% Retail 5% Office
Open Space Place Types					
AGR	Agriculture		N/A	N/A	
F	Forest		N/A	N/A	
OS	Open Space		N/A	N/A	
P	Parks		N/A	N/A	

Source: Sacramento Area Council of Governments.

desktop version is no longer supported by the various developers, although it is still in use by some agencies.

Scenarios are developed using place types based on user-generated assumptions. The tool has around 100 evaluation indicators, including total jobs and dwelling units, density by land use type, a mix of uses (defined by land use type), economic feasibility, vehicle miles traveled and vehicle trips per household, and change in walk/bike and transit mode shares. This information can be examined for each scenario in a report or exported to regional travel models. The indicators for various scenarios or different subareas within a scenario can be compared in a report format.

I-PLACE³S has a built-in ROI function and can estimate water and sewer flow rates. It also has 4D functionality, an energy module that estimates gas and electric energy consumption and emissions, and a health module that estimates health attributes based on urban form. A number of new modules, features, and tool updates have been developed by users including the California Energy Commission and the Sacramento Area Council of Governments.

THE FUTURE OF SCENARIO PLANNING TOOLS

In many ways this report is a harbinger of the future of scenario planning tools. To date, the growth in their use has been primarily in a closed environment, with each tool carving out its own, often proprietary, market silo. These tools generally don't "talk" to one another, so they cannot easily share data or functionality. But this incompatibility is changing as scenario tool developers become more collaborative.

Some of the research in this arena focuses on the creation of generalized modules that can be used by several tools. A module is a self-contained set of analytical methods that addresses a specific set of indicators. For example, a real estate finance module might be developed to calculate a return on investment or residual land value. In the current programming environment it is possible to write such a module so it can be used easily by different software programs. Such a module could be developed once and then used by all the current scenario planning tools (figure 14).

The IPLACE³S infrastructure model and the Envision Tomorrow + 7D transportation modules being developed at the University of Utah are examples of portable methods (or modules) that can be used with other systems or tools. This type of framework approach means that advances to the major scenario planning tools, if they are amenable to open source approaches, could include connections to other applications (both modules and new tools) from developers throughout the world. For example, multiple tools might be connected to advanced visualization engines, such as the Decision Commons at the University of Washington.

Some tools, such as CommunityViz, support limited interoperability by providing ways to import and link data to proprietary and nonproprietary databases and spreadsheets. While this process is currently considered best practice, data and model description standards will help advance a much more seamless level of interoperability. All of the platforms described here are linked with Esri's ArcGIS, although the direction of new entrants in the field points toward a reduced reliance on Esri products (box 2).

Emerging Trends
Four broad trends in information technology also have implications for future applications of scenario planning tools.

The first is crowdsourcing, a nontraditional way to collect data by asking people to

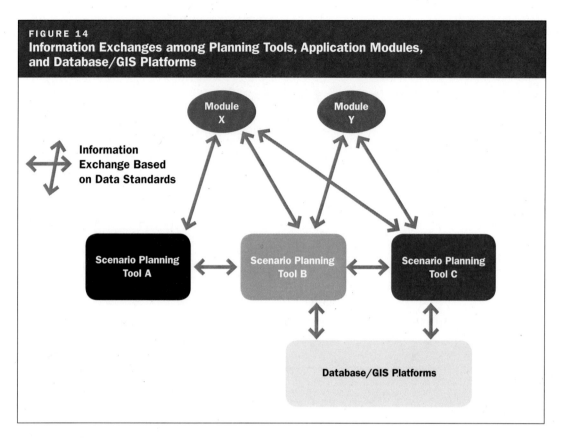

FIGURE 14
Information Exchanges among Planning Tools, Application Modules, and Database/GIS Platforms

Information Exchange Based on Data Standards

Module X

Module Y

Scenario Planning Tool A

Scenario Planning Tool B

Scenario Planning Tool C

Database/GIS Platforms

contribute an item of data, often a personal observation made while going about their normal daily tasks. Online review sites such as Zagat and Yelp are familiar examples of crowdsourced data. Internet-enabled cell phones have greatly increased the opportunity for such data collection. As part of their 311 information services, many cities now have cell phone apps that allow individuals to report graffiti, broken street lights, potholes, and other local concerns. When people encounter a problem, they can note it, take a picture, and, if their cell phone has GPS, record the location. *OpenStreetMap.org* is a website that allows people to contribute spatial information to a freely available map. Crowdsource data can come from voluntary contributions or be derived by monitoring activity patterns in existing city services, such as 311 reports, 911 or complaint lines.

Second, trends in Internet usage point to more people accessing online information by using mobile browsers on their cell phones or other devices rather than on traditional computers (Horrigan 2009; Wortham 2009).

Mobile applications and websites that present planning and scenario issues and analysis will potentially reach many new and untapped audiences

The third trend is the emergence of web-based GIS that can provide powerful mapping and analytical work entirely within a web browser on a computer. Web mapping tools also require less up-front configuration for the end user, and can be easily replicated and updated in multiple locations. As online mapping providers add more functionality and tools to their sites, users will become more familiar with web GIS, and more developers will use web maps as the basis for innovative tools. Applications like Google Earth and MapQuest have already brought GIS tools to the public, and many counties now provide access to county assessor data through such web applications. Planning departments in cities are now beginning to experiment with such systems to deliver information and provide a way for people to contribute their ideas as part of a planning process.

BOX 2
Emerging Tools

In addition to the four major commercially available tools, several others have been released recently or are in development.

Urban Vision

This open source software system is used for visualizing alternative land use and transportation scenarios at scales ranging from individual neighborhoods to large metropolitan areas. It is a server-client system that extends the UrbanSim model to provide an interactive land use and transportation simulation and visualization tool. The simulation outputs include the prediction and analysis of alternative land use and transportation policies and plans, including real estate development and redevelopment at a parcel level. The visualization outputs include interactive views of 3D urban models created automatically from the simulation outputs. The system supports fly-through and walk-through interfaces to allow nontechnical stakeholders to visualize and interpret the nature of the proposed land use and probable outcomes from those simulations.

The project is a collaborative effort between the University of California, Berkeley and Purdue University. It is led by Professors Paul Waddell of Berkeley and Daniel Aliaga and Bedrich Benes of Purdue, and funded primarily by the Metropolitan Transportation Commission of the San Francisco Bay Area, with support from research grants sponsored by the National Science Foundation and Google, Inc.

Decision Commons

Decision Commons is a research initiative of the University of Washington's Runstad Center for Real Estate Studies. The project was created from the desire to design a revolutionary way for urban governments to make decisions around difficult infrastructure and land use issues, with funding from HUD's Sustainable Communities Regional Planning Grant program.

Decision Commons provides cutting-edge, seamless 3D visualization of our cities—from street level to the regional scale—connected to powerful analysis and design tools. The result is the ability to sketch alternative futures quickly and compare them side-by-side. Stakeholders in the planning process will have easy access to relevant information on environmental, social, land use, transportation, real estate, and economic development issues.

This tool can visualize plausible future conditions in 3D and display high-level information through a graphic dashboard to facilitate conversation and understanding of complex problems. The system also supports decision making through an interactive user experience that allows participants to explore scenarios in real time by adjusting designs or assumptions.

Rapid Fire

Rapid Fire was developed by Calthorpe Associates for Vision California, a statewide planning effort funded by the California High Speed Rail Authority and the California Strategic Growth Council to explore the role of land use and transportation investments in meeting the state's environmental, fiscal, and public health challenges. This comprehensive modeling tool has the capability to inform state, regional, and local agencies and policy makers about climate, land use, and infrastructure investment policies. This nonspatial, spreadsheet-based sketch planning tool produces and evaluates statewide, regional, county, and/or city scenarios across a range of metrics. It is based on empirical data and the latest research on the role of land use and transportation systems on automobile travel, emissions, and land, energy, and water consumption.

The model produces results for a range of critical metrics, including vehicle miles traveled; GHG emissions from cars and buildings; air pollution; fuel use and cost; public health impacts; building energy use and cost; water use and cost; land consumption;

and fiscal impacts (revenue, infrastructure and operations and maintenance costs). It provides a single transparent framework within which these assumptions and research can be loaded to test the impacts of varying land use patterns on environmental and fiscal performance. The Rapid Fire model can be run as a stand-alone process or with other models such as Envision Tomorrow.

Urban Footprint

This open source map-based model is also being developed as part of the Vision California process. Built entirely with open source software, it is a scenario creation and modeling tool with co-benefits analysis capacity. It includes a full set of 30+ detailed and researched place types built up from a set of 50+ building types; a scenario translation engine that converts input scenarios into Urban Footprint place types; a scenario "painter" for custom-built scenarios and scenario editing; an 8D travel model; a public health analysis module; climate-sensitive building energy and water models; fiscal impact analysis; and a GHG and other emissions model.

It also produces a wide range of scenario metric outputs: vehicle miles traveled; GHG emissions from cars and buildings; air pollution; fuel use and cost; public health impacts; building energy use and cost; water use and cost; and land consumption and fiscal impacts (revenue, infrastructure and operations, and maintenance costs). Initially, Urban Footprint will be used with the first round of California's Central Valley-focused scenarios.

Finally, as governments move more services and information to online systems, the underlying data should become more available to a variety of potential users. This accessibility to data could also lead to the development of many third-party applications and analyses, which will offer diverse ways to engage with local issues and services. These new applications of the data may extend benefits in previously unanticipated ways. For example, many transit providers publish data about their services in a structured, machine-readable format. Google and other services retrieve data from hundreds of cities to provide transit planning. The same data can also be used by entirely different developers to calculate transit-sheds of service coverage for analytical purposes. As planning-related data such as land use, tax rolls, and other basic elements become available, scenario planning tools will be able to take better advantage of them.

All of these trends suggest that in the near future scenario planning tools will connect more easily to a wider array of information sources and offer expanded opportunities for public engagement in scenario planning processes.

SUMMARY

Over the last 10 years scenario planning tools have advanced substantially and have emerged as a key factor in facilitating the integration of scenario planning within broader planning processes, ranging from site planning to regional visioning. Just as scenario planning is evolving to respond to issues of high uncertainty such as climate change adaptation, scenario planning tools also will evolve in a direction of more flexibility and utility. Yet, if these tools are to continue to expand the use of scenario planning, a number of challenges will need to be addressed.

CHAPTER 4
Challenges to Using Scenario Planning Tools

Residents of Beaverton, Oregon, participate in a scenario planning exercise.

Tool developers and users agree that significant advances are being made in the use and functionality of scenario planning tools, but obstacles to their widespread use remain. The biggest concerns identified by the Lincoln Institute and Sonoran Institute workshop participants are lack of trust in scenario planning and scenario planning tools; complexity and high costs; finding, obtaining, and using relevant data; lack of interoperability across tools; and integrating foresight and anticipation into planning processes.

An informal web-based survey of planners and scenario tool developers was conducted in November and December 2011 as part of the research for this report. Though it was not a scientific survey, 121 respondents shared their experiences and recommendations. The survey explored who was using scenario planning tools, which tools were being used, how they were being used, and what people thought were the barriers to their use (see Appendix).

About one-third of the respondents indicated their organization was using or had used one or more scenario planning tools, and 80 percent of the users indicated their experience was positive or strongly positive. CommunityViz was the most widely used tool among tool users and the most recognized tool among nonusers. City, county, metropolitan (MPO), nonprofit, university, consultant, and tool developer organizations were all represented among the respondents.

MPOs were the most frequent tool users and cities the most frequent nonusers.

The respondents used the tools for a broad range of planning activities, with regional planning, land use analysis, and public engagement being the three most common. Between 40 and 60 percent of tool users and nonusers agreed that the three greatest impediments to using scenario planning tools are high costs, complexity, and the availability of staff resources to support scenario planning. Approximately 20 to 25 percent of both groups ranked availability of data, difficulty integrating different models, and trust in the tools and results as significant barriers.

SKEPTICISM AND LACK OF AWARENESS

Public planning has always struggled to achieve high levels of community participation, particularly for plans that look to the long term. Community residents struggling to keep their heads above water in the current economy are less likely to pay attention to planning issues that do not seem relevant to immediate concerns regarding their jobs or the loss of equity in their homes. Some people do not want any government involvement in planning their future. These skeptical attitudes can be further aggravated by scenario planning tools that may be overwhelming for those not experienced in thinking about complex urban land use and transportation systems.

Distrust and fear of government is an issue that transcends scenario planning, but distrust due to a lack of understanding of the planning process and tools is a challenge that can be addressed. Scenario planning, when performed properly, can contribute to rebuilding trust in government and increasing public engagement on long-term community needs.

The key to improving public support is clear communication with participants in scenario planning activities. The planning profession has a rich history of promoting concepts of customer service and public education, and this experience can be applied to communicating information about scenarios and their implications for the needs of those affected by the planning process.

Acceptance of scenario planning and tools has also been slow among planning professionals themselves. Scenario planning is not typically included in a professional planner's formal education for two reasons. First, its slow adoption by practitioners minimizes its importance for planning schools. Second, many universities are experiencing budget constraints; thus funding development of a scenario planning curriculum, systems, and the tools required to provide hands-on experiences for students has not been a high priority.

The current and potential uses of the tools are focused primarily on regions and large communities that are, or will be, engaged in a long-term visioning or planning activities that seek to explore alternative futures. The number of potential users in the United States is quite large, including approximately 385 MPOs, over 3,000 counties, several hundred cities with populations over 100,000, and a number of place-based nongovernmental organizations. However, the actual number of current users is only a fraction of this potential audience.

Current users of these tools include many of the nation's largest MPOs and planning agencies, yet even among these groups scenario planning tools tend to be employed infrequently. Some agencies use the tools as part of plan updates, while others use them as part of more detailed planning efforts, such as corridor plans and downtown plans. Why is the actual user base so small when the potential is so large? One reason may be the manner in which scenario planning has been implemented.

MPOs and COGs are regional bodies whose members are appointed by agencies and units of government, and they have been reluctant to use market, agent, or stochastic models to predict the location or scale of regional growth and land uses, in part because that would single out particular member jurisdictions with different prospects for growth. Thus, most projections are simple and proportional allocations of estimated regional growth based on each community's existing land use plan. The organizations also have been reluctant to explore scenarios that may result in regional growth patterns that differ from those based on the existing land use policies of their member governments.

Since 2007 the U.S. Department of Transportation has been promoting the use of scenarios in transportation planning at a community and regional scale, resulting

in their inclusion in many planning initiatives (figure 15). Yet the use of scenarios remains unsophisticated. Most cases include basic transportation options such as high or low use of public transit, but only a few explore different forms and patterns of land use development beyond those created by the transportation options (Bartholomew 2007; O'Toole 2008). HUD has recently included a scenario planning requirement as part of its Sustainable Communities grant program.

Only in the last decade with the emergence of regional visioning projects has scenario planning become utilized as a normative planning tool in grassroots efforts initiated outside the traditional planning processes of the MPOs and COGs and in partnerships of regional organizations, such as regional chapters of the Urban Land Institute. Even among these efforts, agreeing on a single vision of the region's future has been difficult. Overcoming the lack of political will needs to be part of any effort to expand the use

FIGURE 15
Build-Out Alternatives for Commercial, Retail, and Housing Uses along a New Light Rail Line in Bellevue, Washington

No Action
Business as Usual

0.9m sf commercial and industrial
124k sf retail

0 housing units

Alternative 1
Mid-Range Housing
Mid-Range Employ.

3.2m sf commercial

300k sf retail

3,500 housing units

Alternative 2
Low Employment
High Housing

2.3m sf commercial

200k sf retail

5,000 housing units

Alternative 3
High Housing
High Employment

4.0m sf commercial

500k sf retail

5,000 housing units

Source: Decision Commons, University of Washington.

Source: Fregonese Associates, Inc.

of scenario planning, particularly at a regional scale.

COMPLEXITY AND HIGH COST

Creating alternative scenarios to represent the possible futures of complex urban systems like land use and transportation is not easy. Scenario tools require a large amount of data to model population, transportation, and land use changes that may occur over time. Since every region is unique, these data must be collected and prepared before the tool can be used for a particular place.

Collecting data, calibrating the tool's models, and structuring the factors that define a scenario are also complicated and require a high level of knowledge about the models themselves and the characteristics of the region or community that will influence its future. Finally, the validity of the scenarios and results are based on the validity of the underlying data and multiple assumptions on policy decisions and other factors that are built into the models.

Using these tools requires a financial commitment to either allocate internal staff resources or hire a consultant to lead a scenario planning process, including the technical work, such as 3D imaging (figure 16). One reason for high costs is the level of experience required to make assumptions about the development or place types that form the basis of the scenarios. A second reason is that many planners find making these sorts of assumptions for future development types to be quite formidable. Planners, for practical and political reasons, often prefer to delegate responsibility to consultants to develop these assumptions.

Most scenario planning tools are built on top of a GIS platform, usually Esri's ArcGIS. For users with minimal GIS experience, running a scenario model can be an intimidating process. Even at the most basic level, these tools require at least one user proficient in GIS. Many smaller municipalities do not have a planner, let alone a proficient GIS user, which is more than a trivial barrier for these communities.

Whether consultant or staff resources are involved, the implementation of the scenario planning tools requires a high level of collaboration. Organizations in which long-range planning, development review, and GIS support are managed in silos find use of scenario planning tools particularly difficult.

The design-based nature of regional and community scenario planning necessitates that those planners skilled in development and policy making help create the scenarios. However, a division frequently exists between the planning staff—who may be managing the development assumptions behind the scenarios, the policy decisions, and the GIS technical work, as well as implementing the scenarios—and those managing the public long-range planning or visioning processes.

Other costs associated with these tools, such as licensing, training, and ongoing maintenance and technical support, typically are not as extensive as staffing and consultant costs. Obtaining a license to use a scenario tool can range from no cost for open source tools such as Envision Tomorrow+ to $1,900 for INDEX PlanBuilder.

All tools require at least some training, and that cost varies depending on existing and desired staff technical capacity. Ongoing technical support and maintenance also vary with each tool and the existing resources of the agency using the tool. For example, I-PLACE³S incurs ongoing data hosting costs since the data live on a remote server. Additionally, most of the current tools require users to have an active license for Esri's ArcGIS.

Even the process of deciding to use a scenario tool can be quite daunting, and opportunities are limited for sharing experiences among regions beyond the most basic process information. The only current forums for tool users to engage in such exchanges are workshop sessions at state and national planning and GIS conferences. Given the absence of standard data sets and outputs and the differences in tool functionality, planning processes, and applications, such sessions rarely go beyond simple comparisons and lessons learned. The absence of a forum where scenario tool users can engage in a detailed exchange of technical information also inhibits widespread understanding and use of these tools.

DIFFICULTIES IN OBTAINING AND USING DATA

Reliable scenario results depend on good input data, so tools need to be calibrated with local data. Ideally, baseline data include parcel-based assessor data and other inputs that contain elements such as housing units, employment types, square footage by use, market value of land, and market value of improvements (Treuhaft and Kingsley 2008). However, the availability and quality of these kinds of data can vary greatly from place to place.

Much of the data being used to create scenarios are free or low-cost and publicly available from government sources, although some agencies are reluctant to make this information available. They may want to protect the privacy of an individual or company, but more frequently this reluctance is rooted in concern over how the data will be used and, for public agencies, what political backlash may occur as a result.

Finding the specific data required for building models is often difficult because there are few common standards among different data locations and creators, and few catalogs for reference. One drawback to the existing large open data catalogs is the difficulty in searching for the most appropriate data. For example, the *data.gov* website contains thousands of data sets on a diverse range of topics and provides filters to narrow the search, but it is often difficult to identify useful data from the vast amount of results available.

Even free data can be challenging to prepare for use in scenario planning tools. Government data are often incomplete or flawed, so planners must spend time "cleaning it up" before use. For example, tabular data may be incomplete or inconsistent. Similar problems apply to geographic data, which have additional challenges if they are stored in diverse map projections, contain duplicate or inaccurate geographic information, or are classified incorrectly. Paul Waddell (2011, 215) estimates "that 75 percent of the effort and an even higher percentage of the time involved in developing model applications is due to the difficulty of developing the data for the model system."

Proprietary data sources can be purchased from commercial firms, such as forecast data from Woods & Poole or consumer and business data from Esri or Claritas. Another emerging source is the delivery of data sets that are ready-to-use, such as a business model called "data as a service" (DaaS). Unfortunately, current scenario planning tools rely heavily on governmental or official data sources and, depending on the tool, it can be difficult to incorporate other, nongovernmental data. Mechanisms to use other forms of data may be particularly important in the future as user-generated data and private data aggregation become more common (figure 17).

Another difficulty is that data publishing from either government or private sources is typically one-way. For example, when a data set of parcel data within a municipality is provided to a planner, he may discover problems in data classification and then clean up the file in preparation for a scenario modeling process. This improved version of the file rarely returns to the original data publisher, where it could benefit future users. Because creating a "round trip"

for user-contributed data is complicated by issues of quality control and verification, few such systems exist.

LACK OF INTEROPERABILITY ACROSS TOOLS

Each scenario tool has different features that can provide advantages for particular aspects of planning processes. Consequently, users often wish to work with multiple tools at different stages in a project. For example, Envision Tomorrow could be used to create scenarios and then CommunityViz may be preferred for the visualization process. Unfortunately, it is difficult for users to change or work across tools once they have

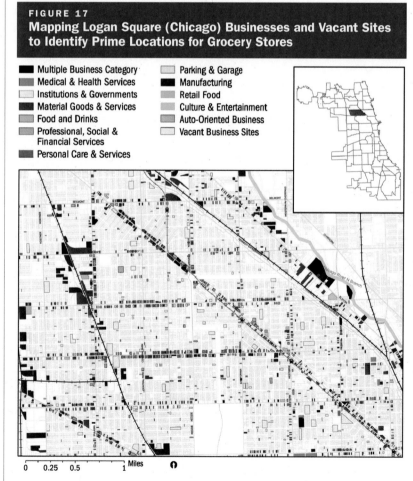

FIGURE 17
Mapping Logan Square (Chicago) Businesses and Vacant Sites to Identify Prime Locations for Grocery Stores

- Multiple Business Category
- Medical & Health Services
- Institutions & Governments
- Material Goods & Services
- Food and Drinks
- Professional, Social & Financial Services
- Personal Care & Services
- Parking & Garage
- Manufacturing
- Retail Food
- Culture & Entertainment
- Auto-Oriented Business
- Vacant Business Sites

Data Source: Chicago Metropolitan Agency for Planning (CMAP), Logan Square Chamber of Commerce. Source: Truehaft and Kingsley (2008, 13).

Community members experiment with land use alternatives for the San Diego region, as part of Our Greater San Diego Vision, an initiative of The San Diego Foundation.

© FREGONESE ASSOCIATES, INC.

created scenarios. There is no common "language" that allows a user to exchange the data created with one tool into another tool. Each of the standards for development of place types used by the tools is different, and each of the tools generates discrete scenario outputs.

Given that the existing tools are mature software products, complete interoperability may not be feasible in the near future. And, while the general state of scenario planning tools is advancing on many fronts, most of these innovations have occurred through competition among tools, not collaboration in the form of modules that are usable across multiple tools. Moving tools toward compatibility is likely to occur only through a more open collaborative development and user environment.

In other software tool areas, such as system utilities, graphics, and GIS, open source software environments have increased both innovation and interoperability. Such environments encourage collaboration and

the development of common data and interoperability standards, but they do not currently exist for scenario planning tools It is unlikely that a single entity would be able to establish a means to embrace the range of organizations involved with scenario planning tools. The process of building a partnership to address these issues will require time, funding, and a commitment to work collaboratively.

NEED FOR FORESIGHT AND ANTICIPATION

The new concept of anticipatory governance suggests using foresight and anticipation to enhance an organization's ability to adapt to change. This new approach to planning has potential to help address issues of high uncertainty such as regional growth and climate change, though its use is just emerging in professional practice and planning discourse. Creating a large number of scenarios and analyzing them in aggregate requires different methods than those used in traditional scenario planning. These methods of scenario generation and analysis are still in their initial stages, and to date have been designed primarily for specific planning projects. Similarly, the scenario analysis tools used for these planning projects were custom built and are generally not applicable to other cases without substantial modification.

Scenario generation and analysis tools used with anticipatory governance are currently at the development stage where the community and regional scenario planning tools were 10 to 15 years ago. Advancement of this concept will require more applied research and application, especially given how different this approach is from customary scenario planning methods. New planning and implementation methods will also have to be developed in order to facilitate incremental applications and adaptation over a long time frame.

Most of the prevalent planning instruments are based on the premise that users can know the future results of their actions. Both traditional and form-based zoning assume that if guidelines are set for how development is to occur, it will occur that way. General and comprehensive plans assume that if an area of the community is designated as parkland or low-density residential, then that use will develop eventually. These are safe assumptions when growth is fairly steady and regulations constrain the market, but in an era of uncertainty and market volatility such assumptions may not be valid.

The economics and public policies associated with land use and development shift dynamically over time. Moving away from a predict-and-plan paradigm and embracing the concept of anticipatory governance will require new thinking with respect to implementation of land use and infrastructure policies. Implementation needs to be designed to facilitate incremental and flexible policy and infrastructure options. Such changes take time, education, and innovative thinking. As scenario planning tools advance, these kinds of changes will support the necessary evolution of planning methods and tools from static to dynamic guidance mechanisms.

SUMMARY

Scenario planning and scenario planning tools have great potential to help communities address issues of high complexity and uncertainty. Yet, the current use of these tools is limited and a number of challenges must be resolved in order to expand their use. For example, the complex tasks of selecting a tool, collecting data, calibrating the tool, developing scenarios, and using the tool to assess various scenarios present significant barriers to many potential users. These challenges do not represent fatal flaws with the concept of scenario planning, but they point to a road map for how the use of scenario planning tools can be enhanced and expanded.

Opportunities to Expand the Use of Scenario Planning Tools

© PLACEWAYS

Participants at a community workshop in Meridian, Idaho, use CommunityViz and ArcGIS with a low-cost interactive sketch table.

A robust array of computer-based scenario planning tools is continuing to evolve to support the use of scenarios with land use, transportation, and other planning needs. However, to reach their full potential, the methods of scenario planning and the current uses of scenario planning tools have to address the formidable challenges described in chapter 4. At the same time, the promise of opening access to scenario planning and the tools that support it through a collaborative open source environment is compelling.

ENCOURAGING ACCEPTANCE OF SCENARIO PLANNING AND TOOLS

People are naturally wary of new ideas or concepts they do not understand, and there is a growing disenchantment with government involvement in problem solving. To overcome these tendencies, planning processes must be transparent and relevant to both community stakeholders and professional planners. Scenario tool developers need to make the inner workings of their tools, including input data and outputs,

38 POLICY FOCUS REPORT • LINCOLN INSTITUTE OF LAND POLICY

easy to understand and adaptable to a community's needs and values. Better educational materials and more opportunities for learning about complex scenario concepts and applications need to be developed for both planners and stakeholders.

Some scenario indicators will be universal to all communities, but accommodation must be made to incorporate particular outputs related to each community's planning process. For example, the urban heat island effect is a growing concern for large southern and southwestern cities, but is not as relevant to smaller northern communities. Tool developers need to provide an easy way for users to customize indicator outputs to match the needs and perspectives of local residents, especially to address emerging and sometimes contentious issues related to community health, economic vitality and jobs, public finance, water supply and demand, social equity, and climate change mitigation and adaptation.

Scenario planning will be viewed as relevant if both planners and the public believe it will make a difference in the community's future. An inventory of case studies would be useful to demonstrate success stories and the various approaches used to conduct scenario planning, with direct links to examples of implementation. Promoting stories of successful projects in professional, trade, and place-specific publications will also help to build public and organizational knowledge of scenario planning.

Exploratory and normative scenario planning methods can help communities address thorny and potentially divisive issues. Thus, if scenario planning and scenario planning tools were institutionalized within existing local and regional planning programs, a wider audience could access the tools through regional joint ventures and other activities that provide services to local communities.

REDUCING COMPLEXITY AND COST

The complexity of scenario planning tools is not likely to be reduced, but they can be made simpler to use through improved interface design, linking of specific tools and models to particular planning processes, and greater sharing of the users' collective understanding of models and successful approaches.

Models require careful configuration to produce useful outputs, but many users do not have the confidence or technical skills to make these necessary assumptions. Guidance and training can reduce the initial "analysis paralysis" and help users get started more easily. A database of case studies that provide technical details on different types of input data, data configuration issues, and libraries of existing development types could be modified for new projects. Users can share this type of information among themselves via informal means such as mailing lists or blogs, or through more formal means such as professional articles and published research.

Most scenario planning tools are built on a GIS platform, usually Esri's ArcGIS. For those with only minimal previous GIS experience, running a scenario model is a complex process. But the tools can be made easier and more intuitive for planners if tool developers could design a user experience that more closely matches the typical work flow of other planning processes. Similarly, the outputs of models could be structured to match the information needed at different stages of scenario planning.

To increase flexibility, scenario planning tools can be moved off a desktop GIS platform and into a dedicated web-based environment, as the Sacramento Area Council of Governments did when it moved PLACE³S to a web platform for I-PLACE³S. Web-based tools may not be as complete as standalone models, but simpler

A class at the Urban Futures Lab at the University of Colorado, Boulder, discusses the scenario planning process.

tools can create reasonably good alternatives with less effort.

Increasing user knowledge of tools will also help to reduce startup and staffing costs. Training for professional planners in the general use of scenario planning and scenario planning tools is critical to getting them started. A focus on the concepts and methods of scenario planning, the features of specific tools, and assistance in choosing among various options would be most helpful. Graduate school programs and professional development courses are ideal opportunities for laying the foundation for advanced tool use in professional practice, but these programs need assistance from planning professionals familiar with scenario planning and from tool developers to create a curriculum and class modules that are relevant to the current and future state of the art.

Starting a scenario planning process is a challenge for many communities and agencies because it entails selecting a tool and possibly a consultant to help set up the tool. Choosing a consultant often involves deciding on a preferred modeling approach

and tool at the same time, so requests for proposals (RFPs) need to describe the model requirements adequately. An archive of RFPs could help users specify a scenario modeling approach for new projects.

Agency adoption of scenario planning tools could also be advanced through regional collaboration and the sharing of expertise, data, and tools. MPOs and other regional organizations or state agencies could support a preferred scenario tool and provide technical assistance to their member agencies. These organizations could also provide basic layers of more standardized types of regional data to help developers create "plug and play" tools to run on this foundation.

Regular user meetings are another way to share and discuss experiences on methods and approaches with different scenario planning tools. Tool developers also have an important role in developing a standard set of simple descriptions of inputs, assumptions, and outputs for each model, thus allowing users to compare tools more easily. In the long term, tool developers could create a standardized report format for model specification and results, and also add functionality to their tools to allow users to create reports themselves. Sharing these reports would aid in comparing various tools and would benefit transparency and portability among tools.

OPENING ACCESS TO DATA

Opportunities to address the lack of available data, quality issues with data, and the cost of data acquisition and setup for scenario planning tools exist at all levels and among all scenario planning stakeholders. Many agencies, public and private, are reluctant to provide data or engage in the effort to organize their data for public planning uses, including scenario planning. Tool developers and users can make the case for increased openness by including demonstrations of the value of data to planning and scenario processes. Moving toward openness does not require intensive new resources. The process can happen gradually and with increasing complexity as organizations develop capacity, and as the demand and willingness to pay for particular data becomes apparent.

As a starting point, public and private agencies can begin sharing their data by placing existing files online for free download and reuse. This will require planners and tool developers to identify the most useful data sets and clearly show the benefits of their use in terms that data providers can appreciate. Data sharing requests will be more successful if they come from several groups, or as part of a collaborative effort including the organizations that control the data.

Finding available information is often difficult because there are few catalogs of regional and community data. To begin developing such a catalog in collaboration with users, data providers, and tool developers, agreement is needed on some basic common standards of metadata, geocoding, and file formats. The use of existing Application Program Interface (API) protocols would allow scenario planning tools to access the most up-to-date databases directly from data providers or through a catalog. Systems such as the Comprehensive Knowledge Archive Network (CKAN) open source data portal software are already being used as a catalog to provide access to data using such an API.

Even after one finds the data sets needed for a particular tool or planning project, the data are often inadequate and require additional effort before they can be used. A new generation of data exploration and cleaning tools has emerged to deal with the growth of big data sets, and they can assist planners in the preparation of models. For example, Google Refine has made it possible to clean up and standardize complex nonspatial data sets, and DataCouch allows users to work on data and then easily share the results.

Most of the data sets used by current scenario planning tools are comparable in structure, so tool developers can create a suite of similar tools to help users clean their data, preferably based on existing open source tools. Ideally, such tools would be designed to interact with data providers to allow a round trip for this data, thereby updating the original data sets so that the next user will not have to repeat this cleaning. This is not a new concept. "Sneaker network" systems are used frequently by COGs and MPOs to allow stakeholder review of their data sets, and peer-reviewed databases are common in the field of bio-research.

ENHANCING INTEROPERABILITY ACROSS TOOLS

Collaboration among tool developers is needed at two levels to enhance the interoperability of scenario planning tools—data exchange and software integration standards. Creating common data standards and file formats for tool input and output data is the simplest way to foster interoperability among scenario planning tools. This collaboration will not only facilitate the exchange of data among the tools, but will also help new tools emerge where a particular capability can be provided.

Collaboration could also focus on developing a standard API for utilizing external applications with scenario planning tools. Many current modeling tools focus on specific aspects of community and regional planning at a place or building level, such as tools for water resources, water and sewer capacity, flood and storm water, fiscal impact, shade, micro climate, viewsheds, and market analysis. Creating a standard API for integrating other applications would allow external applications to be linked into the tools, or at least facilitate the movement of data among the scenario tools and these specific applications. Using these applications to extend the functionality of scenario planning tools could avoid duplicating work that has already been completed and would build on the existing user base and experience of each tool package and application. Establishing a standard API would also encourage third parties to be involved in the design and development of new tool functionality.

Interoperability is not a new idea. Most scenario planning tools already include one or more pieces of software working together, including common components of GIS or spreadsheet functionality, with the scenario tool as a layer on top that provides scenario-specific options (figure 18). Increasing the diversity of layers within this interconnected set of tools provides greater flexibility for users, because they can choose how to

purchase and use each layer individually. In the long-term, portable modules that are compatible with a wide range of scenario planning tools will lead to a comprehensive scenario development toolset with interchangeable parts.

ADVANCING FORESIGHT AND ANTICIPATION

To advance the concept of anticipatory governance, new analysis and regulatory tools will have to be developed by university planning programs, nonprofit policy research groups, and others to address uncertainty and educate future planners in their use. This report focuses on the existing major scenario planning tools for community and regional planning, but advances in scenario planning in other fields may represent the next generation of approaches. Community and regional planners and scenario tool developers need to engage people from these other fields to participate in a broader discussion about scenario planning and the tools that can support it.

FIGURE 18
3D Visualization of a Transit Station Area Build-Out

Source: Decision Commons, University of Washington.

These new methods of foresight and anticipation will not require the development of new modeling platforms in community and regional planning because existing scenario planning tools can be used as a base for added functionality, and modules can be developed to implement new scenario analysis methods. One such method is factor sensitivity, and some tools already have functionality to explore the sensitivity of indicators such as GHG to changes in policy or factors such as density and walkability. How to use various new and evolving functions and analyze the results should be part of scenario planning education and scenario tool training (figure 19).

CREATING AN OPEN ENVIRONMENT FOR COLLABORATIVE ACTION

A common theme in the challenges and opportunities of scenario planning is the need for an open environment for sharing information among various stakeholders, including tool developers, planners, and community residents. Informally, through the Lincoln Institute and Sonoran Institute workshops, an interest group has begun to develop an online resource to help this collaborative effort further organize and expand its activities to create interoperability among existing tools and promote the creation of new tools.

Online resources can help create the open environment for collaborative action. The Internet has proven to be a key facilitator of open source approaches by providing an easily accessed location where people can engage in discussion, exchange ideas and files (data and code), archive information for public use, and otherwise support use of the tools. Web-based platforms allow individuals to collaborate on developing standards in key areas such as data and functionality while adding their expertise and experience

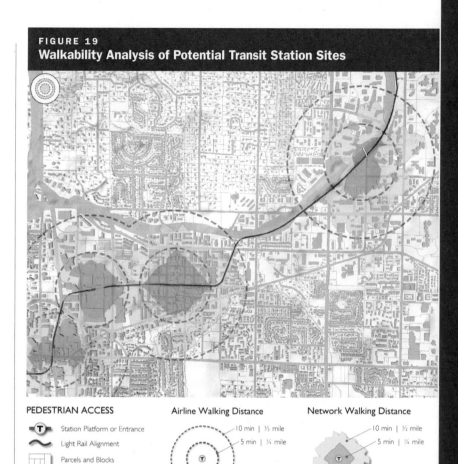

FIGURE 19
Walkability Analysis of Potential Transit Station Sites

PEDESTRIAN ACCESS
- Station Platform or Entrance
- Light Rail Alignment
- Parcels and Blocks
- Right of Way (ROW)
- Streams and Water Bodies

Airline Walking Distance
- 10 min | ½ mile
- 5 min | ¼ mile

Network Walking Distance
- 10 min | ½ mile
- 5 min | ¼ mile

Source: Decision Commons, University of Washington.

to the collective project in a way that can be accessed and used by a wide audience.

Establishing a platform for scenario planning tools will provide a gathering point and information exchange for existing conversations and collaborations. As part of the collaborative environment, online forums and blogs can provide a resource where individual questions are answered in plain sight and past questions can be reviewed in archives. Lists of resources, particularly online resources, could be gathered by users and tool developers to direct people to the information they seek.

Collaboratively edited documents or websites (Wikis) can assemble similar knowledge into online how-to guides, primers, and cookbooks. Efforts to develop and promote standards and interoperability also can be coordinated online. Existing open source scenario modeling projects can use the site to share their resources and coordinate work. The site could be used to organize "App Competition" events to convene planners, government administrators, elected officials, and tool developers to build tools around special issues, such as walkability, health impacts, and other indicators of community sustainability. New audiences will also benefit as the platform would increase the visibility of activities around scenario tools and the potential of open approaches.

Establishing an online resource is only a starting point in encouraging a collaborative environment. The site will require ongoing active participation. All of the information provided has to be contributed and kept up-to-date. Blog posts need to be written, and questions answered. Online tools make these processes easier and bring in a wider

audience, but the website alone will not foster participation. A successful site will require the support of the full range of organizations and people involved in scenario planning practice and scenario tool development and use.

Eventually, a formal consortium body may be required to lead and coordinate efforts. One model for such a body might be the Open Geospatial Consortium (OGC), which promotes standards for geographic data and formats. Another might be OSGeo, which supports open source GIS projects. The effort to create and maintain an online site to focus these activities and provide open access to information will require significant funding, and the organizations and individuals involved in developing, using, and promoting scenario planning tools will need to contribute to developing and maintaining such a website, much like OpenPlans and the Mozilla Foundation do for their efforts.

Participants in the voting process during an App Competition at the San Francisco TransportationCamp event in March 2011.

CHAPTER 6
Recommendations for Action

Expanding the use of scenario planning and scenario planning tools is an important but complex goal that will likely take years to accomplish. Recognizing that many of the issues addressed in this report are highly interdependent, the key is to begin with a manageable set of actions to jumpstart the process. The specific recommendations presented here are either already underway but need additional support, or could be implemented quickly to move scenario planning forward. A community of tool developers, planners, and other users is already working to advance these efforts.

CREATE AN ONLINE PLATFORM TO FOSTER COLLABORATION

A website to host collaboration, capacity building, and open source activities is a first step to address many of the challenges and opportunities facing users of scenario planning and to expand the acceptance and use of scenario planning tools. Such an environment does not exist currently, but through their joint venture the Lincoln Institute of Land Policy and Sonoran Institute are committed to catalyzing this effort by publishing this report and encouraging the establishment of a partnership to fund, design, promote, and maintain an online scenario planning platform for collaboration around both tool building and scenario planning applications.

It is anticipated that this online platform will consist of a catalog and repository for information including documents and code; a system for managing open source and collaborative projects; and a forum to facilitate ongoing discussion including managed blogs, newsletters, and articles. Many

© DECISION COMMCNS, UNIVERSITY OF WASHINGTON

of the necessary resources and tools already exist, but the new online platform will provide a way to combine efforts and focus attention. The platform will not be developed from scratch, but will utilize one of the existing open source collaboration platforms. Additional partners and funders will be necessary to support the coordination and facilitation that will help to move this effort forward.

DEVELOP A CURRICULUM ON SCENARIO PLANNING

To further encourage acceptance of these tools, attention must be focused on educating the next generation of professional and citizen planners. They need to have the knowledge and desire to incorporate scenario planning as part of their community planning projects. A group of participants in the Open Source Planning Tools workshops drafted and submitted a proposal to the Planning Accreditation Board (PAB) to add

Interactive decision making environments provide an ideal setting to train students in the concepts and use of scenario planning tools.

© PLACEMATTERS

Interactive sketch tables, such as this one used at a workshop in Falmouth, Massachusetts, can enhance community engagement in the scenario planning process.

scenario planning to the set of core skills to be included in the curriculum of accredited, degree-granting planning schools.

However, this proposal will require a significant effort for some universities that do not have a formal GIS program, faculty with scenario planning experience, or the funds to develop such a curriculum or purchase and set up scenario planning tools for student use. Thus it is proposed to develop a model curriculum and provide scenario tool access to students at a reduced cost.

This initiative must be a collaborative project among experienced professional planners, university professors who teach planning, and scenario tool vendors. Such a curriculum would include a resource base of education materials and articles; materials covering existing and emerging concepts and application of scenario planning in a lecture format; and problem-solving exercises that use actual scenario planning tools in a studio environment. It will require the creation of prepackaged scenario tool projects that can be used as the basis for studio exercises, and it would be desirable to offer multiple tools so students can gain experience with different tools and their capabilities.

ESTABLISH A MODEL PROCESS FOR SCENARIO PLANNING

Acceptance of scenario planning can also be advanced through a collaborative effort

among regional planning agencies, scenario planning professionals, and tool developers to illustrate how it can be embedded within traditional and nontraditional regional and community planning processes. There are numerous examples of how scenario planning is being used by planning agencies, but most projects have had to start from scratch. A basic model of how scenario planning and existing tools can be used as part of a planning effort would help to accelerate the startup process for regions and communities of various sizes and capabilities.

Such a model will be particularly important as scenario planning becomes a requirement of federal and state planning programs, such as HUD's Sustainable Communities program, or California's Sustainable Communities and Climate Protection Act of 2008, which requires exploring sustainable community strategies as part of regional transportation planning.

Development of such a model for scenario planning use should be based on case studies of existing regional projects and should be a collaborative effort with projects initiated under HUD's capacity-building grants. Such an effort should also include posting the model and related publications and resources on websites such as the Sonoran Institute's SCOTie information exchange.

EXPLAIN THE RELATIONSHIPS BETWEEN TRADITIONAL PLANNING AND SCENARIO PLANNING TOOLS

Professional and citizen planners would benefit from a better understanding of the relationships among different planning processes and available scenario planning tools. This information will reduce the challenges presented by the complexity and cost of the tools and will explain how specific tools and other support systems may be appropriate to facilitate various stages of traditional planning processes.

A relationship diagram in the form of a matrix could list the stages of planning processes, such as visioning, comprehensive planning, and site planning. On the adjacent side of the matrix would be the functions available within specific tools. The matrix cells would identify how each tool function is appropriate for various stages of planning. As part of the online platform, this matrix will be available for use as a standard guide for integrating scenario planning into various planning processes.

ESTABLISH DATA STANDARDS FOR DEVELOPMENT AND PLACE TYPES

Users of existing and future scenario planning tools would benefit greatly from scenario tool input and output standards that allow data sets to be exchanged across tools and among regions, thereby improving access to data needed for effective scenario planning. One such data standard could define a region's urban form. Cities and metropolitan regions within the United States follow similar models of form and function. However, due to factors such as geographic features, community age, climate, culture, economies, and politics, variations in development patterns can be quite distinct from one region to the next.

The current lack of a national classification system for development types requires each community to identify and then define existing and possibly desired future land use patterns in terms of the data factors used by a particular scenario tool. The recommendation is to create a data standard for urban form based on a standard classification methodology and a taxonomy of development forms for various regions across the country. This data set could be used as a starting point for defining a com-

munity's development types, significantly reducing the time and expense required to establish the information on a case by case basis.

INITIATE A COLLABORATIVE PROJECT FOR INTEGRATED TOOLS, MODELS, AND MODULES

Many planners and scenario tool users are interested in incorporating various secondary analysis models and indicators into existing and future scenario planning tools. Much of this interest is related to social issues including spatial population shifts among demographic groups; equity issues in accessing transportation, housing, recreation, and other services (social, health, retail, education); jobs and housing mismatches; and community health issues such as obesity, asthma, and heat. Most of these factors have well-established relationships and metrics that could be coded into models for use with scenario planning tools.

Establishing one or more specific projects in this area will demonstrate ways to enhance

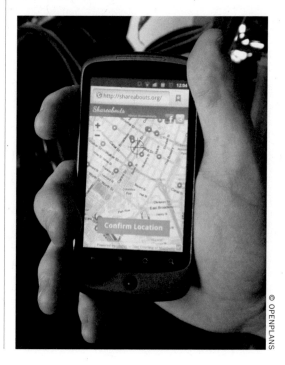

New open source applications could be developed to enable smart phone data entry (crowdsourcing) directly into scenario planning tools.

interoperability by helping the tools talk to each other. Rather than relying on vendors to build their models and indicators independently, the recommendation is to develop modules that can be plugged into different existing and future tools.

This project will require four steps: 1) development of a standard methodology to plug models and/or indicators into scenario planning tools; 2) establishment of a list of plug-in models and indicators that are desired by tool users; 3) development of specialized models and indicators by experts in these fields; and 4) documentation of how these new indicators will be used in scenario evaluation and linked to existing tools.

ADVANCE NEW CONCEPTS TO ADDRESS FUTURE CHALLENGES

Though the concepts of anticipatory governance, foresight, and anticipation are new to the field of community and regional planning, they have the potential to help address highly uncertain factors, such as political will, growth and the economy, market dynamics, and climate change, which currently are not well served by traditional scenario planning methods. These concepts should be incorporated into the ongoing development and use of scenario planning and tools.

Three promising areas are: 1) including the concepts of foresight and scenario analysis in scenario planning training workshops as a method of exploratory scenario planning; 2) convening researchers and practitioners to discuss the concepts of anticipatory governance and how current implementation instruments (such as capital facility planning and programming, zoning, subdivision ordinance, travel demand management, budgeting, public finance, and building design) could be modified to accommodate long-term, flexible, and robust implementation strategies; and 3) convening tool developers and researchers to discuss new methods and tools that are needed to support anticipatory scenario analysis within existing community and regional scenario planning.

SUMMARY

Scenario planning is a valuable method to help regions and communities understand and plan for their futures under highly complex and uncertain conditions. Though scenarios have been used as a planning tool for almost 50 years, their adoption by community and regional planning agencies has been slow for a number of reasons. The emergence of new and improved scenario tools over the last 10 years offers promise that the pace of scenario planning use can increase and that the goal of providing open access to the full potential of scenario planning capabilities is within reach.

The kinds of uncertainties we face are not driven primarily by short-term phenomena and most likely will increase over time. We need to establish methods that will enhance our ability to adapt to change and build flexible management mechanisms into our planning processes and tools well before such change becomes critical. This report suggests that a number of challenges remain, but numerous opportunities also exist to address these challenges in the near and long term.

GLOSSARY

3D
A three-dimensional image, typically of a building, streetscape, or city.

3D, 4D, 6D, 7D, 8D Travel Models
Travel models that can estimate the trip reduction resulting from changes in the various Ds of a project or community: Diversity, Density, Design, Destination Accessibility, Distance to Transit, Development Scale, Demographics, and Demand Management.

AB 32
California Assembly Bill 32: Global Warming Solutions Act. Adopted in 2006, it sets goals for GHG emissions by 2020.

Anticipatory Governance
This new approach to planning suggests using foresight and anticipation to enhance an organization's ability to adapt to change.

API
Application Program Interface is a definition that software programmers can use to design their software to interact with other software.

ArcGIS
This flagship GIS software product sold by Esri provides both spatial data management and analysis as well as map-making tools.

CAD
Computer-aided design software is used primarily by engineers and architects.

Co-benefits Analysis
This type of analysis identifies unanticipated secondary benefits of a policy or action.

COG
Councils of Governments are regional quasi-governmental agencies located throughout the United States. Local governments join them as a way to coordinate their activities at a regional level.

Crowdsourced Data
Data is voluntarily collected by people as they go about their normal daily activities.

Data as a Service (DaaS)
This concept refers to the Internet-based delivery of data on demand by a data consumer, independent of when and where the data is requested.

Esri
Environmental Systems Research Institute, Inc., a GIS software company.

Exploratory Scenario
A scenario that is used to explore the implications of a possible future on predetermined goals and values.

Fly Through
A computer software-based visualization that enables one in real time to rapidly move about a 3D image, as if flying through the actual place.

Geocoding
The identification of the three-dimensional location of an object, frequently in terms of its longitude, latitude, and height, so that its location can be displayed on a map or globe.

GHG
Greenhouse gas emissions are gases released into the atmosphere that absorb and emit radiation within the thermal infrared range.

GIS
A geographic information system is computer software used to create and manage geocoded information, as well as analyze data spatially and create maps of such data.

Main Street
A software program used to indicate a streetscape that looks similar to a small city's downtown main street.

Metadata
A description of the information that is stored in a database.

MPO
Metropolitan Planning Organizations are designated by the U.S. Department of Transportation to plan the transportation system of a metropolitan region.

Nonspatial
Information that is not associated with any specific geography.

Normative Scenario
A scenario used to help identify a desired future.

Open Source
Software whose source code is available for free.

Planning Accreditation Board
An appointed board of the American Institute of Certified Planners that determines accreditation for university planning programs based on a set of standards. It is cosponsored by AICP, the American Planning Association, and the Association of Collegiate Schools of Planning

Platform
A basic set of general purpose software functions that are used to build larger software applications. For example, operating systems such as Windows and Apple's OS X Lion provide basic file support used by other applications to read and write files. ArcGIS and other open source GIS platforms provide basic GIS functions that can be used to provide GIS capabilities in other applications.

ROI
Return on Investment is a tool for financial analysis.

SB 375
California Senate Bill 375. The goal of this bill is to reduce GHG emissions from cars and light trucks. It requires development of a sustainable communities strategy for achieving emissions reduction targets.

SketchUp
A Google software tool that can be used to quickly sketch a 3D computer image.

Spatial
Information that describes a geographic location.

Viewshed
The geographic description of the span of landscape that can be viewed from a particular location.

Walk Through
A computer software-based visualization that enables one in real time to move slowly about a 3D image, as if walking through the actual place.

REFERENCES

Bartholomew, K. 2007. Land use-transportation scenario planning: Promise and reality. *Transportation* 34(4).

Brail, R. K. 2008. *Planning support systems for cities and regions.* Cambridge, MA: Lincoln Institute of Land Policy.

Brewer, G. D. 1983. Some costs and consequences of large-scale social systems modeling. *Behavioral Science* 28(2): 166–185.

Condon, P. M., D. Cavens, and N. Miller. 2009. *Urban planning tools for climate change mitigation.* Cambridge, MA: Lincoln Land Institute of Land Policy.

Cox, P., and D. Stephenson. 2007. A changing climate for prediction. *Science* 317(5835): 207–208.

Flyvbjerg, B., M. K. S. Holm, and S. L. Buhl. 2005. How (in)accurate are demand forecasts in public works projects?: The case of transportation. *Journal of the American Planning Association* 71(2): 131–146.

Holway, J. 2011. Scenario planning tools for sustainable communities. *Land Lines* 23(4) October: 7–13.

Hopkins, L. D., and M.A. Zapata (Eds.). 2007. *Engaging the future: Forecasts, scenarios, plans, and projects.* Cambridge, MA: Lincoln Institute of Land Policy.

Horrigan, J. 2009. *Wireless internet use.* Pew Internet & American Life Project, Washington, DC: Pew Research Center.

Innes, J. E., and D. E. Booher. 2010. *Planning with complexity: An introduction to collaborative rationality for public policy.* New York, NY: Routledge.

Krishnamurthy, S. 2005. An analysis of open source business models. In *Perspectives on free and open source software,* eds. J. Feller et al. Cambridge, MA: MIT Press.

Kwartler, M., and G. Longo. Visioning and visualization: People, pixels, and plans. Cambridge, MA: Lincoln Institute of Land Policy.

Lempert, R. J., and M. E. Schlesinger. 2000. Robust strategies for abating climate change. *Climatic Change* 45(3-4): 387–401.

Milly, P. C. D., J. Betancourt, M. Falkenmark, R. M. Hirsch, Z. W. Kundzewicz, D. P. Lettenmaier, and R ,J. Stouffer. 2008. Stationarity is dead: Whither water management? *Science* 319(5863): 573–574.

National Research Council of the National Academies. 2010. *America's climate choices: Panel on adapting to the impacts of climate change.* Washington, DC: The National Academy Press.

Nielsen, M. 2012. *Reinventing discovery: The new era of networked science.* Princeton, NJ: Princeton University Press.

O'Toole, R. 2008. Roadmap to gridlock: The failure of long-range metropolitan transportation planning. *Policy Analysis* (617), 28.

Pielke, R. A. Jr., D. Sarewitz, and R. Byerly Jr. 2000. Decision making and the future of nature: Understanding and using predictions. In *Prediction: Science, decision making, and the future of nature,* eds. D. Sarewitz, R.A. Pielke Jr., and R. Byerly Jr. Washington, DC: Island Press.

Quay, R. 2010. Anticipatory governance: A tool for climate change adaptation. *Journal of the American Planning Association* 76(4):496–511.

Riehle, D. 2007. The economic motivation of open source software: Stakeholder perspectives. *IEEE Computer* 40(4): 25–32.

Sonoran Institute. 2012. Successful Communities Online Toolkit. *http://scotie.sonoraninstitute.org*

Southern California Association of Governments. 2009. White paper: Conceptual land use scenario methodology. CA Senate Bill 375. *http://www. scag.ca.gov/sb375/pdfs/CLUS_WhitePaper063009.pdf*

Stewart, T. 2000. Uncertainty, judgment, and error in prediction. In *Prediction: Science, decision making, and the future of nature,* eds. D. Sarewitz, R.A. Pielke Jr., and R. Byerly Jr. Washington, DC: Island Press.

Superstition Vistas Consulting Team. 2011. *Superstition Vistas: Final report and strategic actions. www.superstition-vistas.org*

Taleb, N. N. 2007. *The black swan: The impact of the highly improbable.* New York, NY: Random House.

Truehaft, Sarah, and G. Thomas Kingsley. 2008. Transforming community development with land information systems. Cambridge, MA: Lincoln Institute of Land Policy.

Vision North Texas. 2010. North Texas 2050. Dallas, TX. *http://www.visionnorthtexas.org/regional_summit/North_Texas_2050.pdf*

Waddell, P. 2011. Integrated land use and transportation planning and modeling: Addressing challenges in research and practice. *Transport Reviews* 31(2): 209–229.

Walker, D., and Daniels, T. 2011. *The planners guide to CommunityViz: The essential tool for a new generation of planning.* Chicago, IL: Planners Press.

Weber, K. M. 2006. Foresight and adaptive planning as complementary elements in anticipatory policymaking: A conceptual and methodological approach. In *Reflexive governance for sustainable development,* eds. J. P. Voss, D. Bauknecht, and R. Kemp. Northhampton, MA: Edward Elgar Publishing.

Wortham, J. 2009. Mobile internet use shrinks digital divide. *Bits,* July 22. *http://bits.blogs.nytimes. com/2009/07/22/mobile-internet-use-shrinks-digital-divide*

RESOURCES

For additional resources and updated information, visit *www.scenarioplanning.io*.

California High Speed Rail Authority
www.cahighspeedrail.ca.gov

California Strategic Growth Council
www.sgc.ca.gov

Carpe Diem West Academy
http://carpediemwestacademy.org

Claritas
www.claritas.com

CommunityViz (Placeways)
http://placeways.com/communityviz
http://placeways.com/communityviz/gallery/
* casestudies/pdf/GrandJunction.pdf*
http://placeways.com/communityviz/gallery/
* casestudies/pdf/BostonCollege.pdf*

Comprehensive Knowledge Archive Network (CKAN)
http://ckan.org

Consensus Building Institute
www.cbuilding.org

Criterion Planners
www.crit.com

Decision Commons University of Washington
http://decisioncommons.org/Decision_Commons.html

Envision Tomorrow +
http://metroresearch.utah.edu/current-projects
www.wasatchchoice2040.com/resources/tools/
* envision-tomorrow-plus*

Esri
www.esri.com

Fregonese Associates, Inc.
www.frego.com

INDEX
www.crit.com

I-PLACE³S
www.sacog.org/services/I-PLACE3S/

Lincoln Institute of Land Policy
www.lincolninst.edu

MapWindow
www.mapwindow.org

Metropolitan Research Center University of Utah
http://metroresearch.utah.edu/current-projects

OpenPlans
http://openplans.org

Open Source Initiative/Open Source Licenses
www.opensource.org/licenses

OpenStreetMap
www.openstreetmap.org

Orton Family Foundation
www.orton.org

OsGeo
www.osgeo.org

PlaceMatters
www.placematters.org
www.smartgrowthtools.org

Placeways
http://placeways.com

PLANiTULSA
www.planitulsa.org/whichwaytulsa/background/scendev

Rapid Fire and Urban Footprint Calthorpe Associates
www.calthorpe.com/scenario_modeling_tools

Sacramento Area Council of Governments
www.sacog.org

SLEUTH
www.ncgia.ucsb.edu/projects/gig

Sonoran Institute
www.sonoraninstitute.org

Southern California Association of Governments
www.scag.ca.gov

Successful Communities Online Toolkit and Information Exchange (SCOTie)
www.SCOTie.org

Superstition Vistas
http://www.sonoraninstitute.org/superstition-vistas.html

TransportationCamp (a project of OpenPlans)
http://transportationcamp.org

Urban Footprint *(see Rapid Fire)*

UrbanSIM–Urban Vision
www.urbansim.org/Main/WebHome

Vision North Texas
www.visionnorthtexas.org

What If?
www.whatifinc.biz/about.php

Woods & Poole
www.woodsandpoole.com

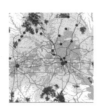

APPENDIX

SCENARIO PLANNING TOOLS SURVEY

Researchers at the Sonoran Institute conducted a survey to assess the opinion of planners who have and have not used scenario planning tools. Ninety-six people responded to an open invitation in the American Planning Association's online Interact newsletter posted on December 20, 2011. Twenty-five people who participated in the November 2011 Open Source Planning Tools workshop responded to an email request, for a total of 121 responses. This survey was intended to be a simple gauge of opinions, not an accurate estimate of planner attitudes in general.

SURVEY QUESTIONS AND RESULTS

Has your organization used (or is your organization currently using) a scenario planning tool?

	#	%
Yes	51	42.1
No	60	49.6
Unsure	10	8.3
Total	121	100.0

How did you use the scenario planning tools? (Users only)

	All Tool Users	
Tool	#	%
Neighborhood Planning	17	33.3
City Planning	18	35.3
Regional Planning	31	60.8
Land Use Analysis	27	52.9
Transportation Planning	19	37.3
Public Engagement	25	49.0
Visualization	22	43.1
Other	1	2.0
N	51	

Which of the following scenario planning tools have you used or are aware of?

	All Respondents		Users		Nonusers	
	Used or Heard of Tool		Used Tool		Heard of Tool	
Tool	#	%	#	%	#	%
CommunityViz	73	60.3	26	51.0	47	67.1
Envision Tomorrow	17	14.0	10	19.6	7	10.0
Index	13	10.7	11	21.6	2	2.9
IPLACE³S	12	9.9	7	13.7	5	7.1
MetroQuest	10	8.3	3	5.9	7	10.0
What If?	11	9.1	4	7.8	7	10.0
None	15	12.4	0	0.0	12	17.1
Other	1	0.8	3	5.9	1	1.4
N	121		51		70	

Please rank the importance of each barrier to using scenario planning tools.

Barrier Ranked 1st or 2nd Highest	Users		Nonusers	
	#	%	#	%
Cost of tools	20	39.2	32	45.7
Complexity of tools	21	41.2	43	61.4
Availability of staff resources	22	43.1	25	35.7
Availability of data	12	23.5	17	24.3
Difficulty integrating different models or platforms	7	13.7	19	27.1
People trusting the tools and/or their results	10	19.6	14	20.0
Communicating the results of the tools	4	7.8	14	20.0
Unnecessary for my organization's work	0	0.0	3	4.3
N	51		70	

How would you describe your overall experience with scenario planning tools? (Users only)

Rank	#	%
Strongly Positive	16	38.1
Positive	19	45.2
Neutral	4	9.5
Negative	3	7.1
Strongly Negative	0	0.0
Total	42	

What is your primary role in your organization?

	Users		Nonusers	
	#	%	#	%
Technical - GIS	5	14.3	1	2.1
Technical Planning	15	42.9	21	43.8
Management	13	37.1	18	37.5
Faculty	1	2.9	1	2.1
Other	1	2.9	7	14.6
N	35		48	

What type of organization do you work for?

	Users		Nonusers	
	#	%	#	%
City	3	7.7	25	52.1
County	3	7.7	8	16.7
MPO	12	30.8	0	0.0
NonProfit	4	10.3	1	2.1
University	2	5.1	4	8.3
Consultant	9	23.1	9	18.8
Tool Developer	5	12.8	0	0.0
Other	1	2.6	1	2.1
N	39		48	

ACKNOWLEDGMENTS

The co-authors particularly wish to acknowledge our fellow participants in two Open Source Planning Tools workshops on scenario planning tools. This report and the larger effort to advance scenario planning exist because of the enthusiasm, creativity, experience, and commitment of the individuals listed below. We also appreciate the assistance provided by our workshop hosts: the University of Utah's Metropolitan Research Center for the November 2011 workshop in Salt Lake City and the U.S. EPA Region 8 for the November 2010 workshop in Denver.

In addition we are indebted to the following colleagues who assisted with multiple aspects of preparing this report.

For reviewing the text:
- Eliot Allen, Criterion Planners
- Armando Carbonell, Lincoln Institute of Land Policy
- Fernando Costa, City of Fort Worth
- Peter Pollock, Lincoln Institute of Land Policy
- Raef Porter, Sacramento Area Council of Governments
- Doug Walker, Placeways
- Karen Walz, Plan for Action

For editing and project management:
- Ann LeRoyer, Lincoln Institute of Land Policy
- Paula Randolph, Sonoran Institute
- Mia Stier, Sonoran Institute

For assisting with graphics and photos:
- Sonya Bastendorff, Fregonese Associates
- Mike Eastland, North Central Texas Council of Governments
- Cameron Ellis, Sonoran Institute
- David Thornton, City of Grand Junction

WORKSHOP PARTICIPANTS

Marina Alberti, University of Washington

Eliot Allen, Criterion Planners

Bruce Appleyard, University of Utah

Anubhav Bagley, Maricopa Association of Governments

Mark Butala, Southern California Association of Governments

Elisa Campbell, University of British Columbia

Armando Carbonell, Lincoln Institute of Land Policy

Randy Carpenter, Sonoran Institute

Chad Coburn, Capital Area Council of Governments

Ted Cochin, U.S. EPA, Office of Sustainable Communities

Joe Concannon, Sacramento Area Council of Governments

Pat Condon, University of British Columbia

Sonny Condor, Portland Metro

Alexander Dane, National Renewable Energy Lab

Karen Danielson, University of Nevada, Las Vegas

Chuck Doneley, Doneley Associates

Cameron Ellis, Sonoran Institute

Reid Ewing, University of Utah

Brenda Faber, Fore Site Consulting/Trust for Public Land

Fletcher Foti, University of California, Berkeley

Larry Frank, University of British Columbia

John Fregonese, Fregonese Associates

C.J. Gabbe, Fregonese Associates

Gordon Garry, Sacramento Area Council of Governments

J.P. Goates, University of Utah

Frank Hebbert, Open Plans

Andy Hill, Colorado Department of Local Affairs

Jim Holway, Sonoran Institute

Alex Joyce, Fregonese Associates

Sarah Kavage, Urban Design 4 Health

Dick Klosterman, What If?, Inc.

Andrew Klotz, RPI Consulting

Matthew Krusemark, Denver Regional Council of Governments

Elaine Lai, U.S. EPA Region 8

Jason Lally, PlaceMatters

Jon Larsen, Wasatch Front Regional Council

Frank Lenk, Mid-America Regional Council

Andy Li, Wasatch Front Regional Council

Nathan Lindquist, City of Rifle

Jill Locantore, Denver Regional Council of Governments

Tracey MacDonald, Colorado Department of Transportation

Debra March, City of Henderson, NV

Robert Matthews, University of Washington

Joe Marlow, Sonoran Institute

Terry Moore, ECO Northwest

Arthur C. Nelson, University of Utah

Robert Paterson, University of Texas, Austin

Peter Pollock, Lincoln Institute of Land Policy

Raef Porter, Sacramento Area Council of Governments

Ray Quay, Arizona State University

John Reinhardt, IBM

Bill Roper, Orton Family Foundation

Nathaniel Roth, University of California, Davis

Randall Rutsch, City of Boulder

Ken Snyder, PlaceMatters

Witt Sparks, National Renewable Energy Lab

Tim Stonor, Lincoln Institute of Land Policy

Carlos Vanegas, Purdue University

Doug Walker, Placeways

Mike Walsh, MetroQuest

Tim Welch, Ecotrust

Garlynn Woodsong, Calthorpe Associates

Li Yin, University of Utah

Thomas York, Criterion Planners

ABOUT THE AUTHORS

C.J. Gabbe, an urban planner with Fregonese Associates in Portland, Oregon, has had a key role in a number of scenario planning projects using Envision Tomorrow, including Superstition Vistas in Arizona and PLANiTULSA in Tulsa, Oklahoma. Previously he worked for the Portland Development Commission and as a staffer to U.S. Senator Ron Wyden. He has a Master of Urban Planning degree from the University of Washington.

Frank Hebbert is the director of civic works at OpenPlans in New York City, a nonprofit organizations using technology to change the way cities and citizens interact. He also co-organizes Planning Corps, a network of volunteer planners who provide assistance to nonprofits. He has a Master in City Planning degree from Massachusetts Institute of Technology.

Jim Holway directs the Babbitt Center for Land and Water Policy at the Lincoln Institute of Land Policy and previously directed Western Lands and Communities, a joint program of the Sonoran Institute and the Lincoln Institute. Prior to joining the Sonoran Institute, he was a professor of practice in sustainability at Arizona State University and assistant director of the Arizona Department of Water Resources. He has a Ph.D. in regional planning from the University of North Carolina.

Jason Lally is the director of the Decision Lab at PlaceMatters, a nonprofit organization based in Denver, Colorado, that works with communities and regions to bring more information to planning and sustainability decision making. He holds a Master in City Planning degree from the University of Pennsylvania.

Robert Matthews is project director for the Decision Commons initiative in Seattle, a joint project of the University of Washington's Runstad Center for Real Estate Studies and the Quality Growth Alliance. His current research is focused on the integration of urban information systems, geospatial analysis, rapid urban modeling, real-time urban visualization, and geodesign. He holds a Master of Urban Planning degree from the University of Washington.

Ray Quay is a research professional at the Decision Center for a Desert City, a National Science Foundation–funded Decision Making Under Uncertainty Center within the Global Institute of Sustainability at Arizona State University. He was previously the assistant director of planning for the cities of Phoenix, Arizona, and Arlington, Texas. He has a Ph.D. in Environmental Design and Planning from Arizona State University.